Sandra Peters
Chromed Columns
Abu Dhabi City

HATJE
CANTZ

Contents

Reflections

On the Chromed Columns / Abu Dhabi City

Sandra Peters

Photography has long played a salient role in my art. The genesis of my three-dimensional works—be they drawings, models, sculptures, or larger installations—almost always begins with photographic documentation of my surroundings, in most cases, the urban spaces through which I move in on a daily basis. I integrate some of these photographs into my exhibitions, where they are typically small and inconspicuous next to larger sculptural works even as they often encapsulate the leitmotif of an exhibition or illuminate the development of a particular work.

In the present book, the relationship between photography and sculpture is, so to speak, reversed. This publication is a reflection on sculpture via photography. Each of the photographs presented within it depicts one or more of the chrome-plated reflective columns that are a characteristic feature of the urban landscape of the United Arab Emirates (UAE), which appear especially often in downtown Abu Dhabi. The columns shown here may be architectural details— but since my initial encounters with them it has become clear to me that they can also be experienced as sculpture.

Reading books about Abu Dhabi is one thing. But as soon as one walks out of the airport, one is welcomed by a hot and humid climate, the air saturated with the scent of oud. Only during the winter months, beginning in mid-November, is it pleasant to spend time outdoors. For half a year, beginning in mid-March, life moves into air-conditioned indoor spaces. The summer heat is compounded by very high humidity on account of Abu Dhabi's location on an island on the shore of the Arabian Gulf. The city forms the northern border of the Emirate of Abu Dhabi, most of which is a vast desert. Its neighbors are Saudi Arabia to the south and west and Oman to the east. The many green spaces in the city owe their existence to the vision of Sheikh Zayed, the first president of the United Arab Emirates following its founding in 1971, who created Abu Dhabi as a garden city.

In 2014, I successfully applied for a professorship in art at New York University Abu Dhabi. I arrived from Berlin in July, which is to say, during the height of summer. My first contact with the city was with the hotels and their lobbies, restaurants, various shopping malls, and museums. As urban infrastructure, all these public spaces, including the airport, are perceptually similar: They are transitional spaces in which most of their users spend limited time. The commercial offerings, too, are uniform: The malls have stores that sell goods from major brands as well as cafés and restaurants that are branches of chains found all over the world. In these environments, hotels, restaurants, and shops with an individual touch are comparatively rare.

Having spent the first few months staying at a series of hotels, I eventually found an apartment on the thirty-fifth floor of the World Trade Center (Residential Tower) in the old city center, in downtown Abu Dhabi, close to the Corniche, facing the Arabian Gulf. It is the city's tallest building. Its footprint has a gently undulating circular outline, and its facade is correspondingly defined by convex and concave segments. The building's top is sloped, so it looks a bit like a calligrapher's bamboo quill. The facade is entirely glazed from top to bottom.

To familiarize myself with new surroundings, I like to go for long walks and document what I encounter. Taking photographs facilitates a gradual approach to the unfamiliar. In Abu Dhabi, however, I could not initially experience the city in this way: Even in September, it was still too hot to spend any time outdoors. Moreover, I had been warned that taking pictures of government buildings was prohibited. At first, it was not easy to distinguish which buildings I was or was not allowed to photograph. So, for the first several months, I concentrated on just walking and observing the urban scene.

Prior to the 1960s, no more than a few buildings stood on the island of Abu Dhabi. Electricity, sewers, and roads were largely nonexistent. People made a living by fishing, diving for pearls, and growing dates. Oil was discovered in 1958; its extraction began in the 1960s; and Abu Dhabi was developed into a modern city under Sheikh Zayed after he became its ruler in 1966.

Two architects, first Katsuhiko Takahashi from Japan, and then Abdulrahman Makhlouf from Egypt, were commissioned to draw up a master plan for the transformation of historical Abu Dhabi and its surrounding islands into a densely populated contemporary metropolis. The designs were modeled on cities in the United States, as the scholar Khaled Alawadi has documented in his studies of urban planning in the UAE.

Abu Dhabi is based on a checkerboard plan that is further structured and given its particular character by superblocks, each of which is made up of an outer ring of buildings rising up to twenty stories, with lower residential and business buildings of no more than six stories behind them. The superblocks are largely self-enclosed units that exist in a dynamic relationship to the larger network of the city grid. Each of them contains at least one mosque and small shops that can be reached on foot and cater to people's daily needs, while the ground floors of the outer buildings have storefronts facing the street.

Much of the city on Abu Dhabi Island was built in the 1980s. The characteristic structures of the period are fifteen-to-twenty-story buildings, usually on square footprints, the majority with mirrored windows and facades incorporating Arabic design elements such as intricate geometrical patterns and arches evoking traditional Islamic architecture. The natural island was soon completely built up, and land reclamation projects were implemented to create a ring of artificial islands for additional development.

More recently, new housing estates have also sprung up on the mainland; some have been completed, while others remain under construction. Buildings from the 1990s and 2000s are considerably taller and have completely mirrored facades. Their designs recall the skyscrapers erected in places like San Francisco, New York, and Chicago from the mid-twentieth century on. Standing out from this mix of building types are specimens of what is known as landmark architecture: examples include Jean Nouvel's Louvre, Frank Gehry's Guggenheim, and the Zayed National Museum by Foster + Partners in the museum district on Saadiyat Island.

Many small shops still exist on street level in downtown Abu Dhabi: They have not (yet) been driven out of business by the large ultramodern shopping malls. Hamdan Street, one of Abu Dhabi's oldest throughfares, runs next to the building complex known as Central Market; it connects the historic fort Qasr Al Hosn with the road leading directly to Saadiyat Island. Named after Emirati politician Sheikh Hamdan bin Mohammed Al Nahyan, it is a popular shopping street with wide sidewalks and a broad variety of stores. Hamdan Street is like a mall without a roof or air conditioning. The majority of the people one meets there are expats who have come to Abu Dhabi for work.

It took a while before I was able to "see" my new surroundings. At first, I was flooded with too many impressions and it was difficult for me to perceive an aesthetic that was foreign to me at the time. Something that caught my eye right away in the urban fabric around me were the many reflective surfaces. Most floors are polished to a shine so that they bring to mind smoothly glistening bodies of water. Windows made of mirrored glass reflect the bright daylight back into the urban space. The visual stimuli produced during the day by the many different surfaces reflecting one another are replaced at night by countless streetlamps, store lighting, lavish advertising panels, and illuminated billboards.

On my walks—at first, I stuck to the major thoroughfares—I noticed an architectural element that reappeared everywhere: chrome-plated round or semicircular columns. They are so widespread, so characteristic of Abu Dhabi's urban scene, that they become almost invisible among the many reflective surfaces wherever one looks. In 2018, four years after my arrival, I decided to document these columns. Questions that initially preoccupied me were: Where does this element appear with particular frequency? What is the specific quality it adds to the urban experience of Abu Dhabi? How does the mirrored surface interact with the other reflective materials like the floors or the mirrored glass facades? I also find it fascinating that the mirrored column, which made its debut in the architectural vocabulary of the 1980s, has remained integral to local architecture and is also present in recently completed large complexes on Reem Island and elsewhere.

At first, I assumed that the columns might be meant to signal to people that they were in the city center—although Abu Dhabi does not have a city center, properly speaking. Like many other modern metropolises, it has various centers for diverse activities and demographics. The columns are sometimes load-bearing and sometimes decorative. They often appear on office and commercial buildings such as hotels, banks, shopping malls, and chain restau-rants, though not only there. Small shopkeepers, too, integrate round, semicircular, or occasionally angular columns plated with chrome into their storefronts. Architecturally speaking, the columns belong to both the structure and the sidewalk. In other words, they exist in a zone between the building's interior and the public streetscape. Some of the columns reflect what is arrayed for sale on the shelves of a shop, resulting in a decontextualization and super-imposition of the object or commodity and the activities in the street; others produce distorted images that absorb the motion of passing pedestrians and cars and project it back into urban space.

Bizarre superimpositions of interior and exterior spaces emerge. Especially when the columns are directly part of the facade, the boundary line of the storefront is breached, and the product seems

to leave the shopwindow. In this liminal situation, the object is
visually uncoupled from its place inside the store, and enters into
the perception of pedestrians. On an unconscious and largely
passive level, they are triggered to register the free-floating object
and, ideally, to want to have it. The effect is not unlike that of an
advertisement intruding unasked into the visual field. On Hamdan
Street, the chromed columns line up ad infinitum, putting pedestrians in a closed loop of encounters with themselves, with the mirror
images of the objects, and with the reflections of life unfolding in
the street.

The columns are usually set by a building's entrances and on its
corners. Larger buildings also feature them at regular intervals
along their facades. The buildings' upper stories are always covered
with mirrored glazing; the shopwindows on the ground floor with
unmirrored glass. By virtue of this materiality alone, the pedestrian's
view differs from that of someone *inside* a high-rise building. In
the chrome-mirrored column, however, these different experiences
are fused. Like the mirrored glass that creates a reflection of its
surroundings on a building's facade, the chromed columns project
everything in their immediate surroundings back into the environment, as images. At street level, they relate directly to the passersby
who are reflected in them, as is the incessant passing traffic. Now
and then I spot columns that look like palm trees, an effect produced
by stepped cornices at their top ends that remind me of streets with
tree-lined sidewalks.

I wonder to what extent the reflective surfaces, the chrome-mirrored
columns, the reflecting facades virtualize the urban experience by
failing to establish the means by which I am usually able to develop
a connection with a particular place. The reflective surfaces, by
both absorbing the unceasing motion of the city and projecting it
back into the urban landscape, offer little opportunity to experience
a "counterpart" in the built environment. I have even had to admit
that it is virtually impossible for me to remember many of these
places because the perpetual reflections make it hard for me to recall
the specificity of the urban fabric. Only the sense of flow I register as
a somatic experience. The homogenization of space that I initially
noticed in the airport, hotel lobbies, and shopping malls effectively
continues in the reflective surfaces and in urban life in general.

When I started photographing the columns, I took pictures from a
distance and tried capturing the facades together with the columns,
which typically appear in series. After initially taking landscape-
format photographs, I started framing the shots in portrait format
so I could get closer to the columns themselves. The portrait format,

moreover, emphasizes the column's function as an element struc-
turing the building on the level at which the pedestrian encounters
it. In several pictures, I focus, in almost zoom-like fashion, on the
mirror images appearing in the chromed columns through which
the urban space is in dialogue with its reflection.

Arriving in Abu Dhabi, I was overwhelmed not only by the culture,
of which I knew little, and the climate, which was utterly unlike
what I was used to, but also by the way people (do not) look at each
other. Although I have become accustomed to it, I vividly remember
how unfamiliar this different culture of the gaze was. For example,
I do not look at men, and when I catch someone looking at me,
I return only women's and children's gazes. Generally speaking, eye
contact is kept more indirect; Looking someone directly in the eye
feels aggressive and disagreeable. The reflections in the columns
resemble the indirect gaze; they are mediators, without establishing
genuine contact. They reproduce experiences that I have in the
city—but I am made anxious by the ways in which their blankness
precludes any dialogue.

Over the course of the many months, years by now, in which I have
been photographing the different columns in their various settings,
I have often considered how they remind me of sculptures. Their
sculptural potential was reinforced by the pictures I took. At first I
was deliberately and consciously extricating columns from their
surroundings when selecting a segment of a scene and recording it
with the camera. But I have now reached the point where I can look
at a column in the cityscape and see it as a sculptural object without
isolating it from its existing context. This shift in my perception
came about through my work taking photographs.

In this book, readers encounter the column as a serial object.
Turning its pages, they see continually varying configurations of
the same element in different locations in Abu Dhabi's urban
landscape. A kind of temporal or spatial sequence emerges, as
though the beholder were walking the same streets I walked to
photograph the columns. But that is an illusion: The serial quality
evoked in this book does not exist in a comparable sequential
density in the streetscape. Registering a recurrent aesthetic feature
in Abu Dhabi's urban fabric, and challenging the distinction
between architecture and art, the photographs instead suggest that
fragmentation and reflexivity are not only at the center of my
personal encounter with the city but also constitutive of the local
experience of everyday life.

Chromed Columns
Abu Dhabi City

01

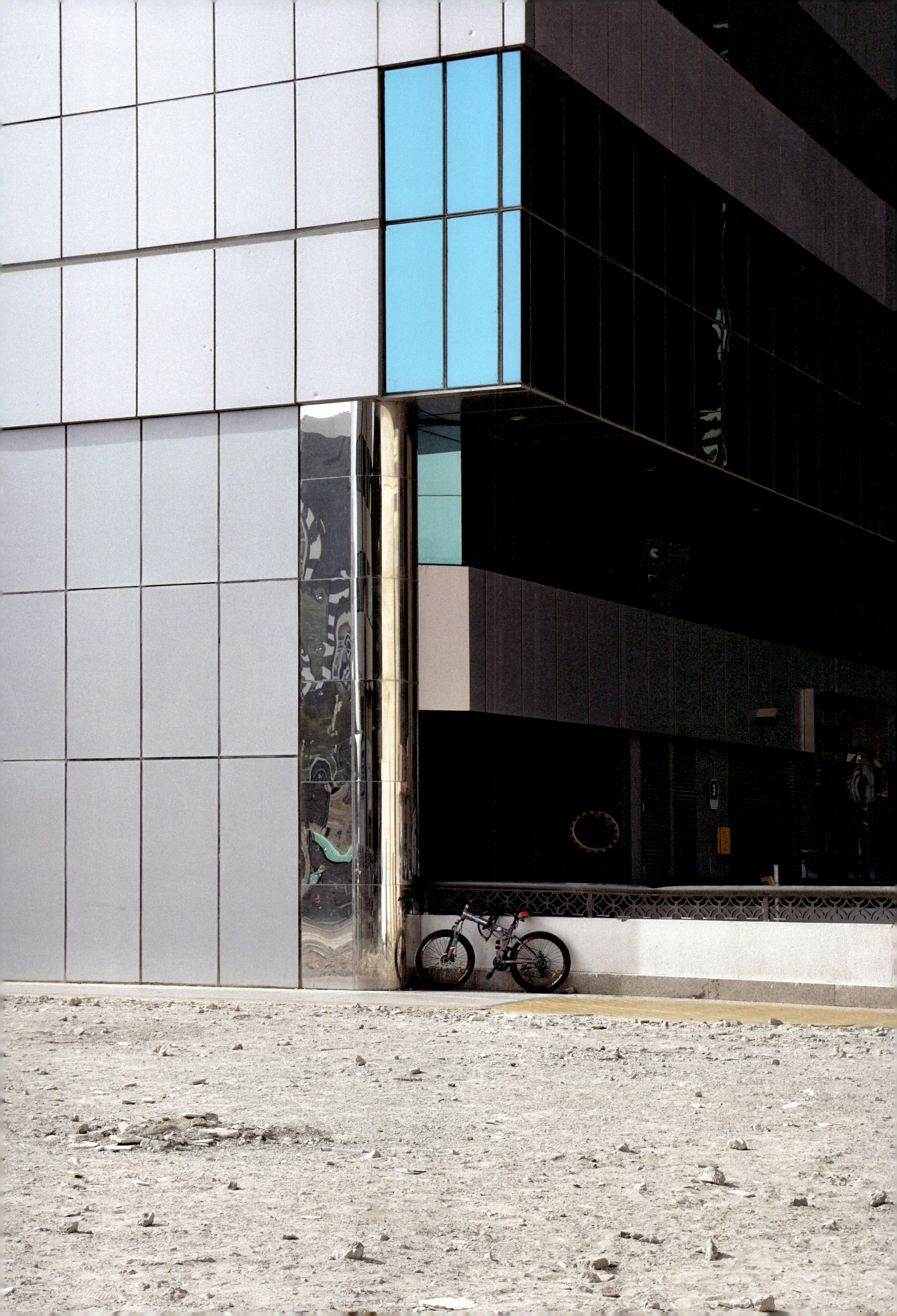

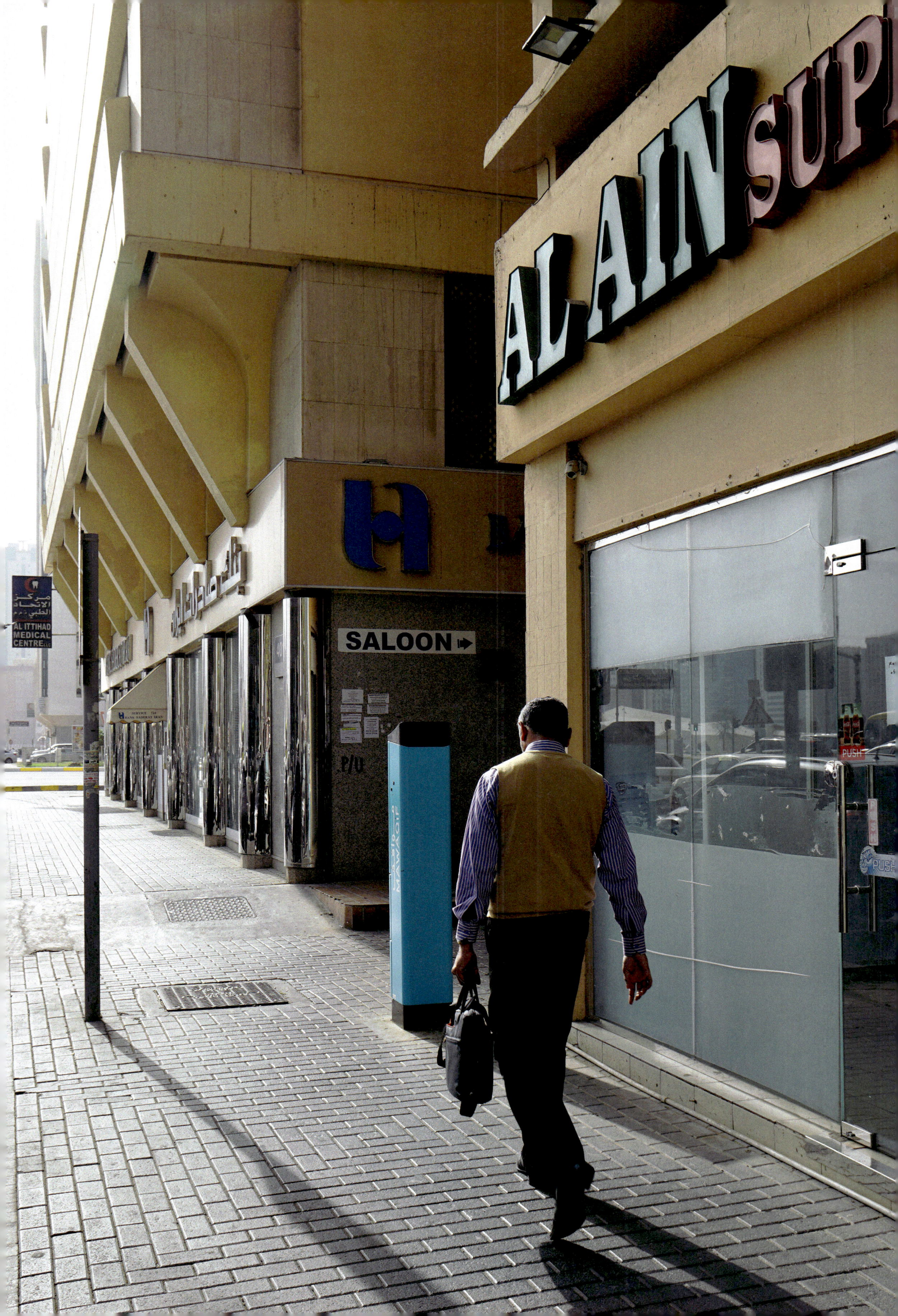
AL AIN SUP
SALOON
AL ITTIHAD
MEDICAL
CENTRE
PUSH
PUSH
P/U

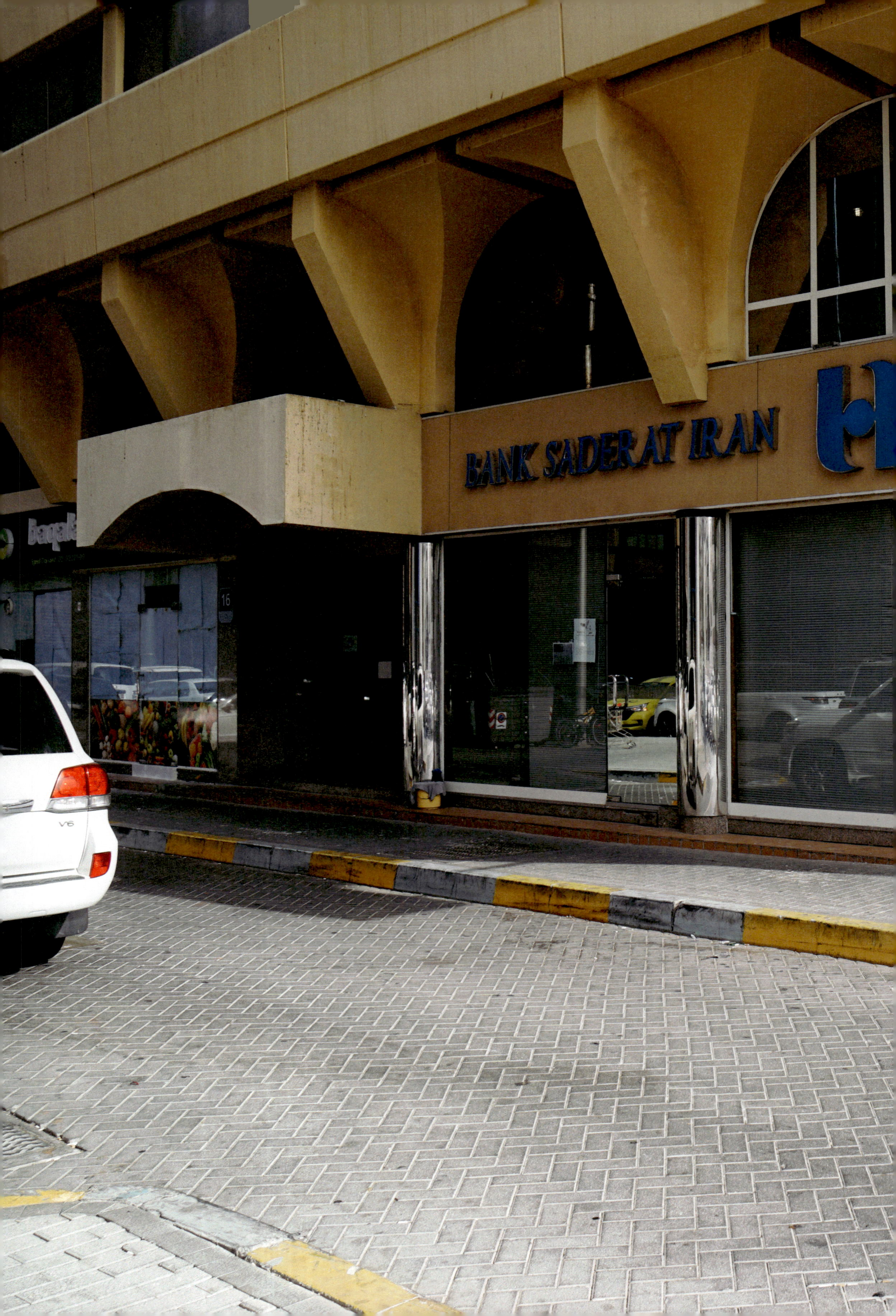

BANK SADERAT IRAN
16

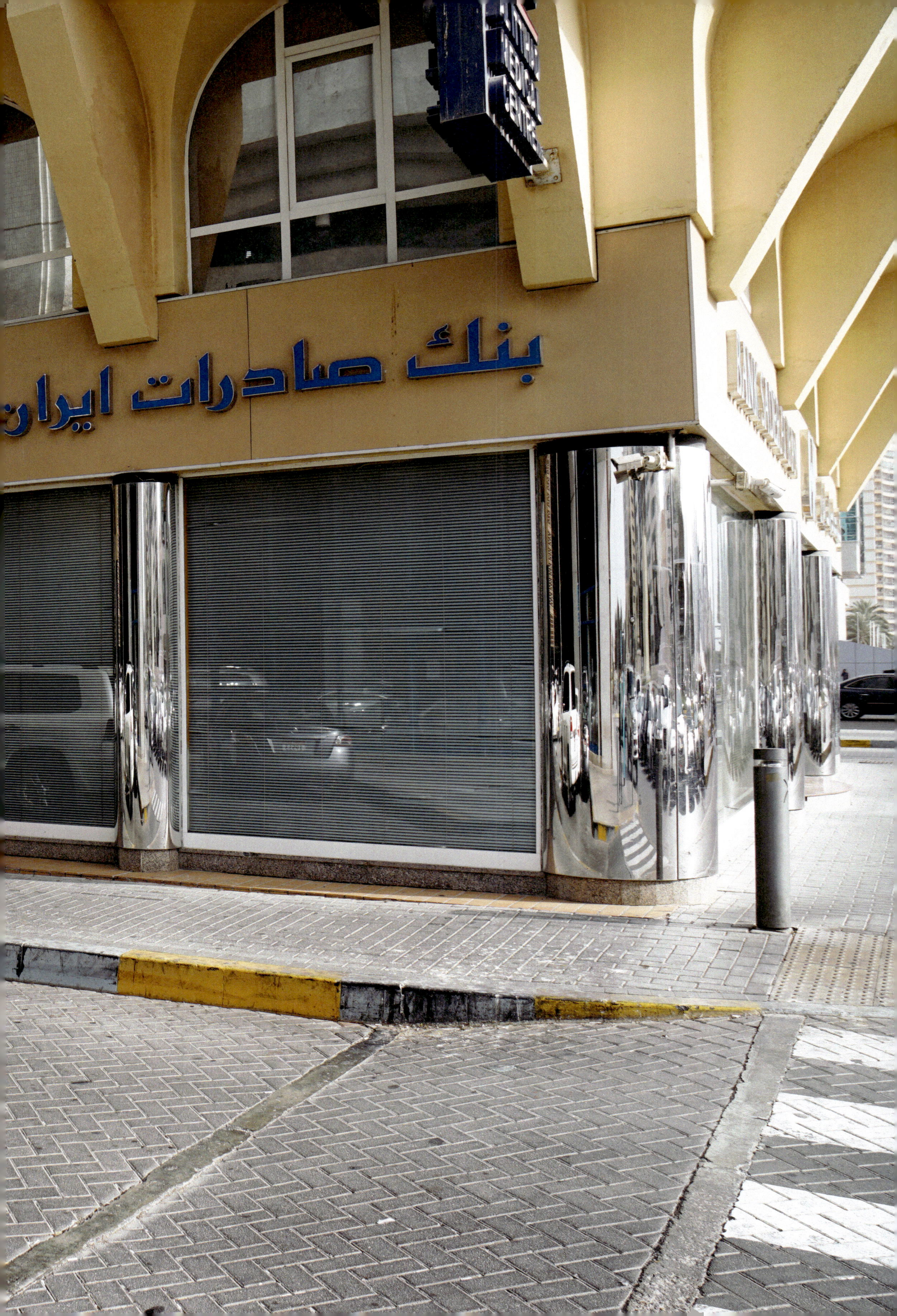
بنك صادرات ايران

← 03
04

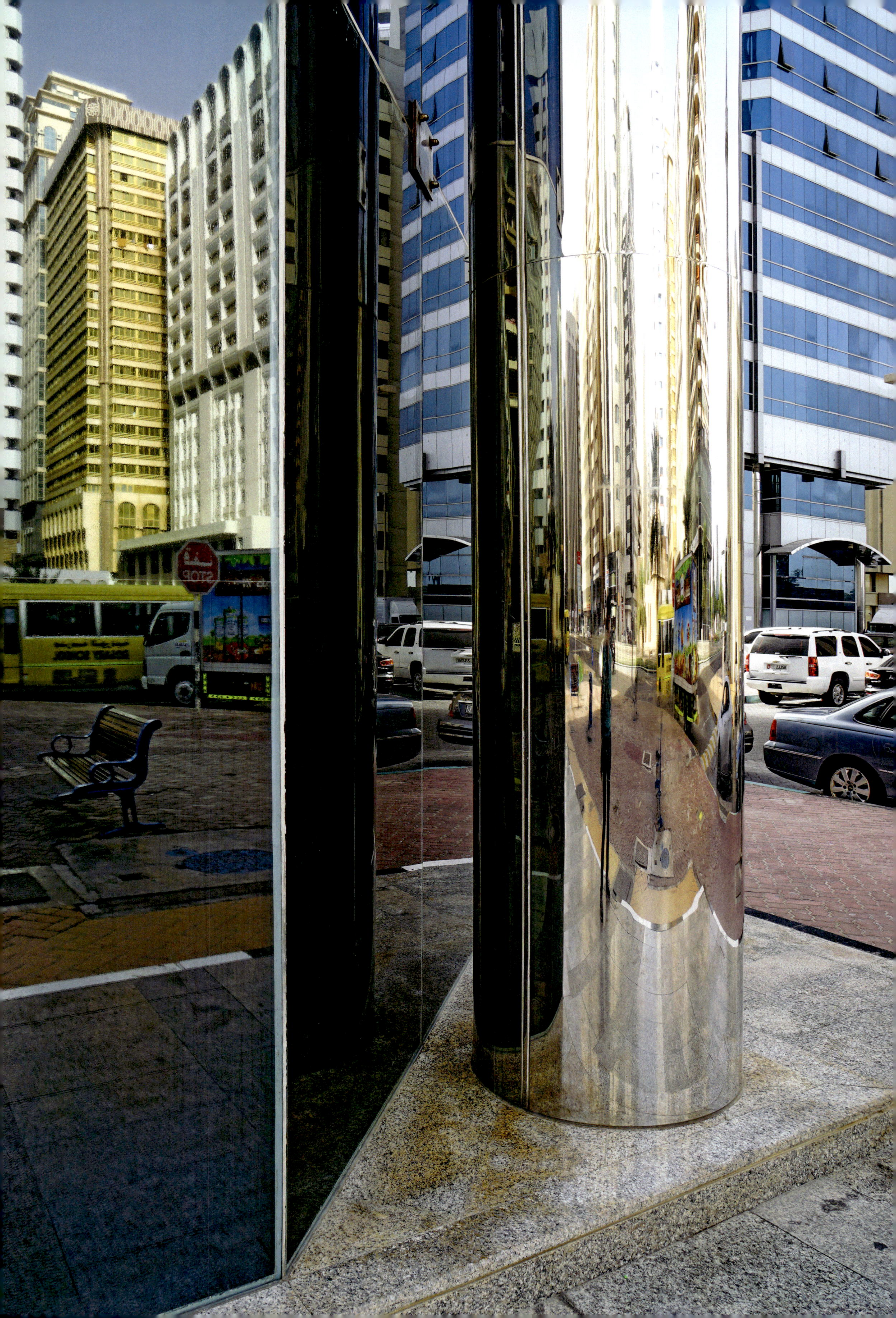

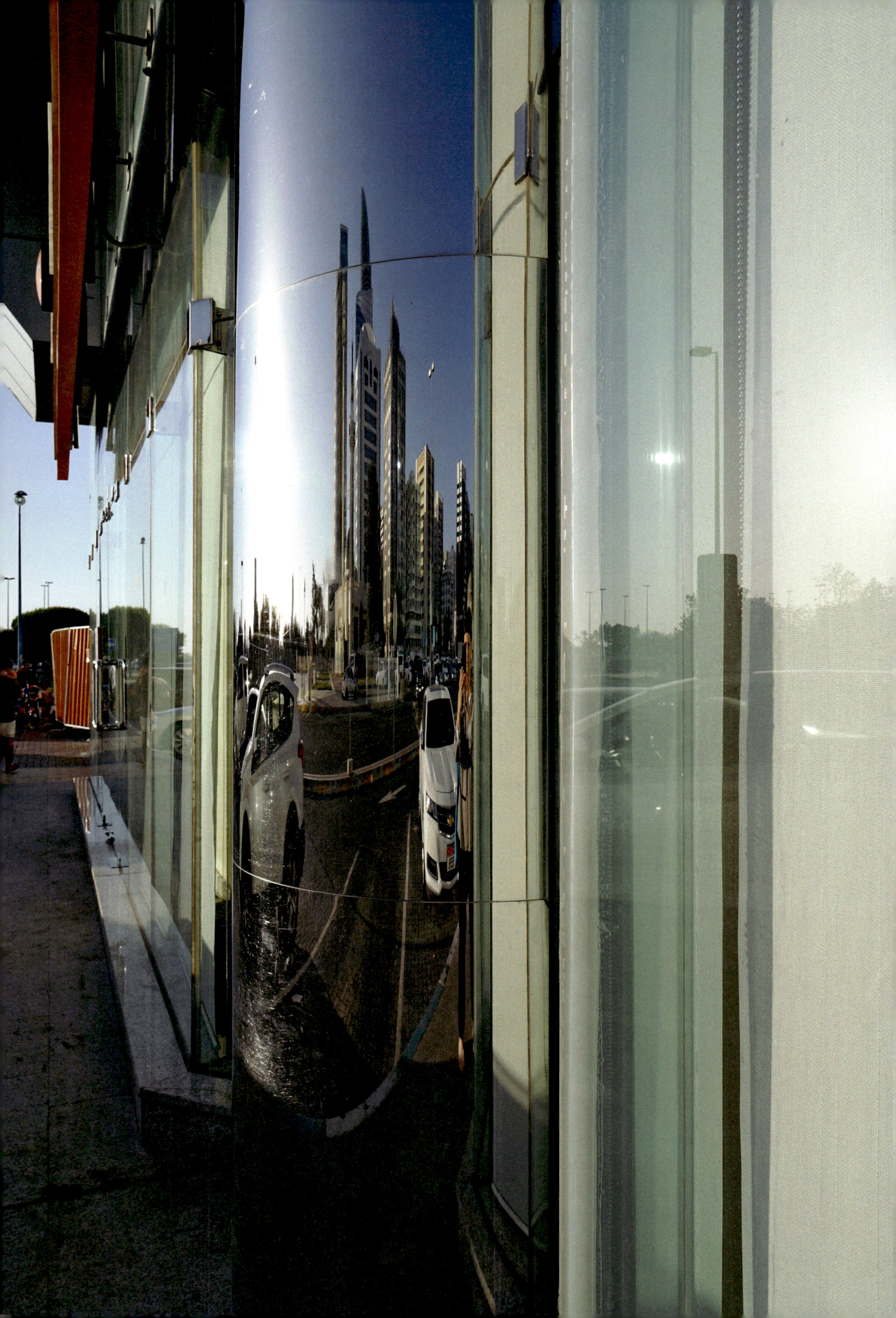

06

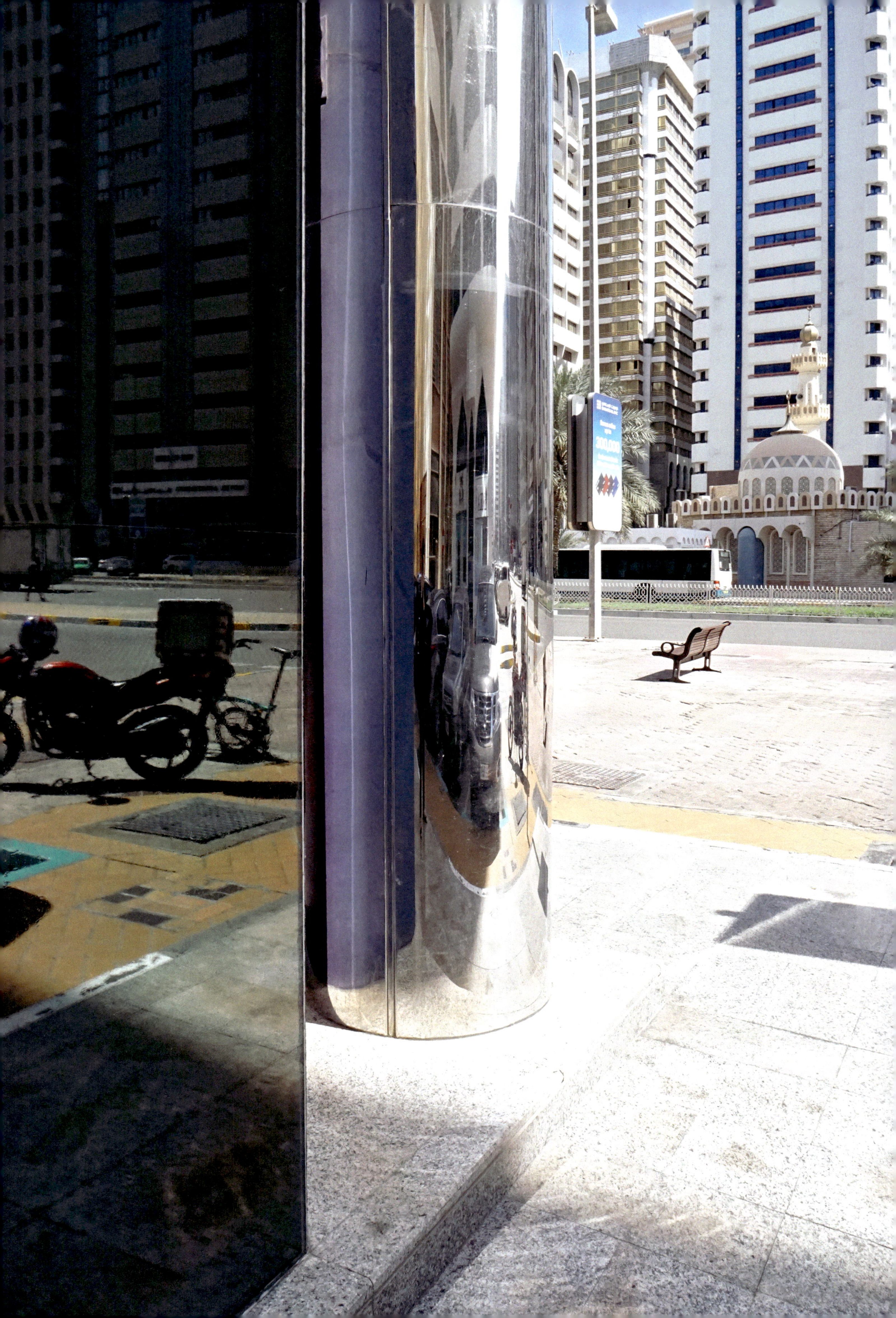

07

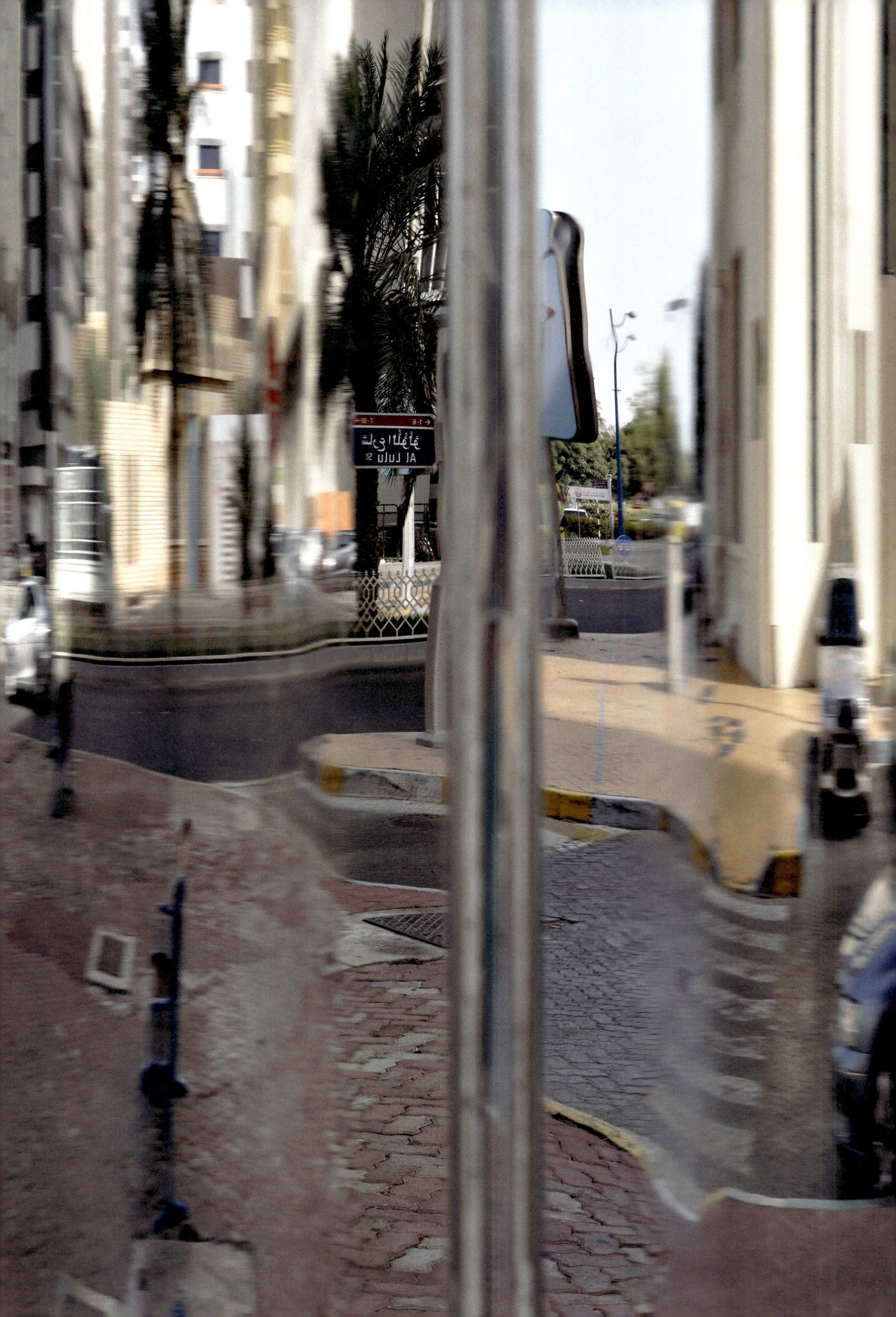
AL Lulu St
شارع اللؤلؤة

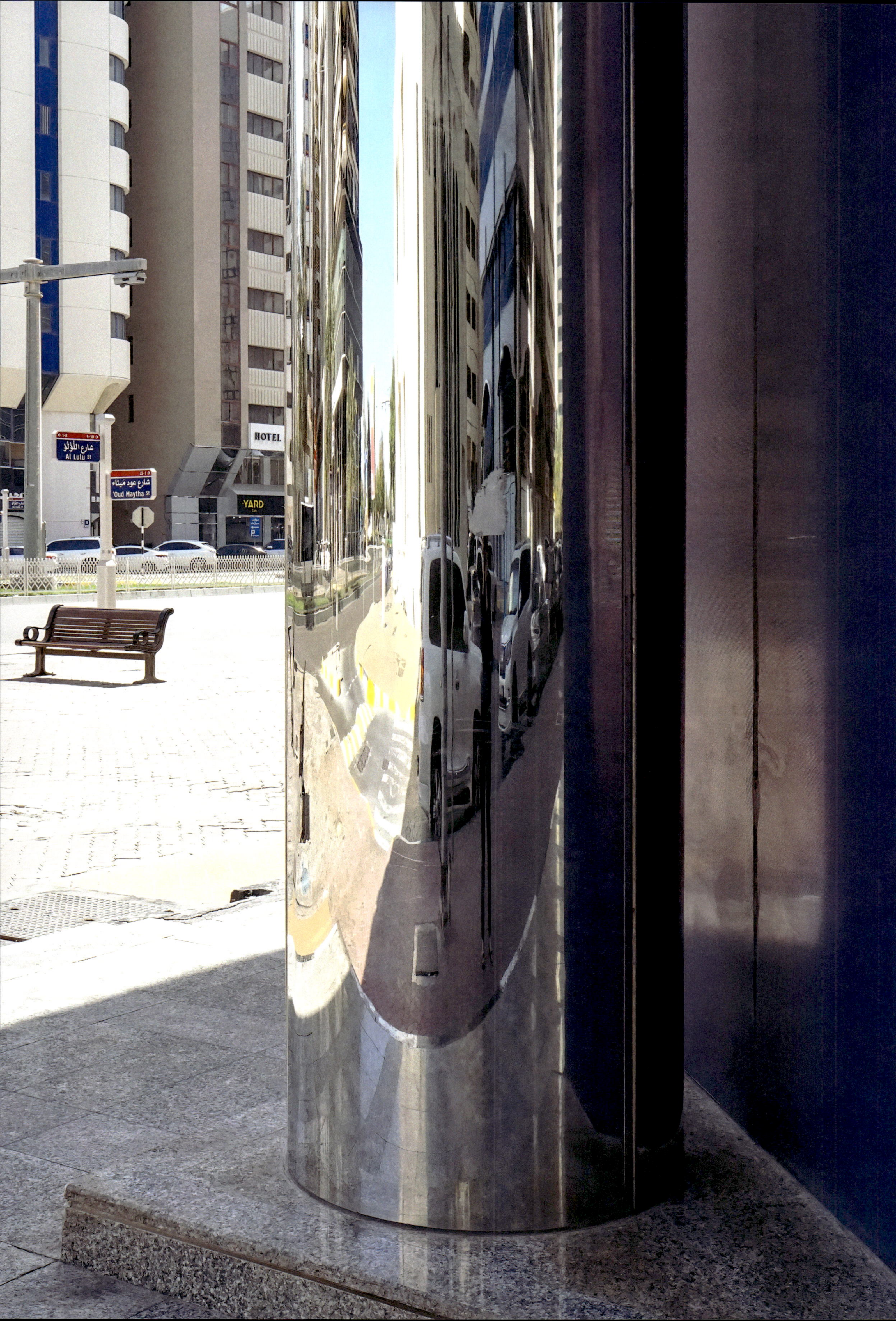

شارع اللؤلؤ
Al Lulu St
شارع عود ميناء
'Oud Maytha St
HOTEL
YARD

09

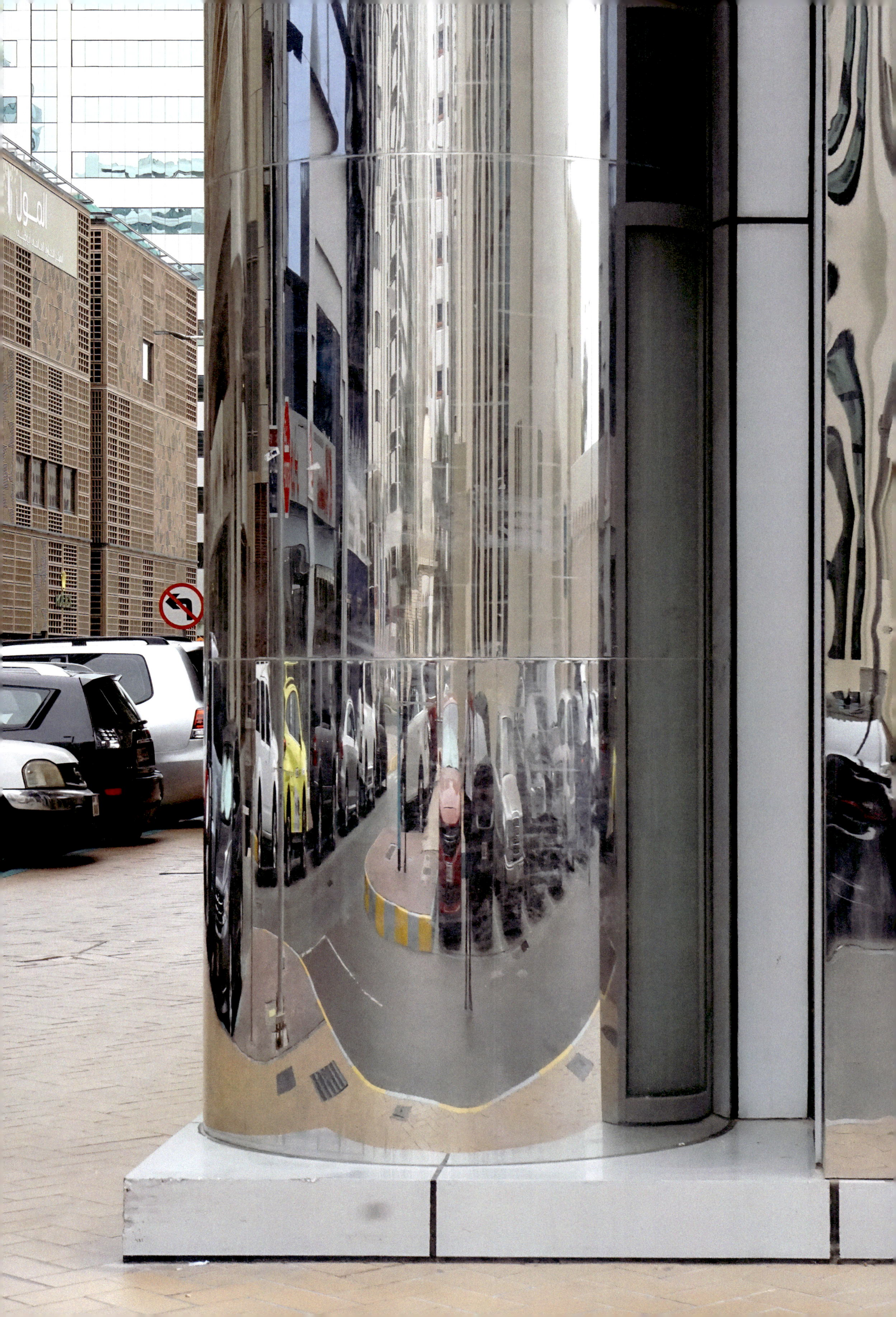

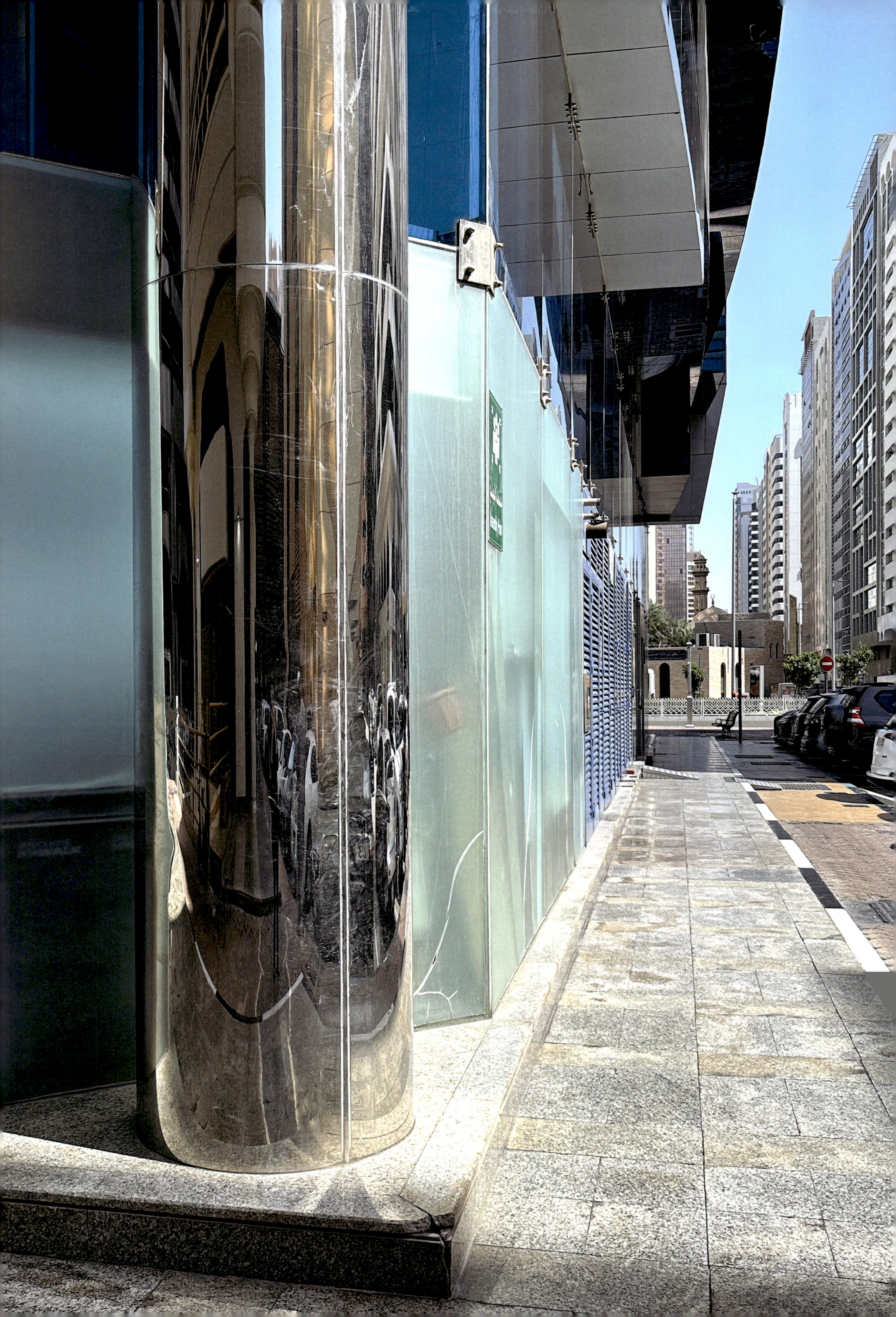

11

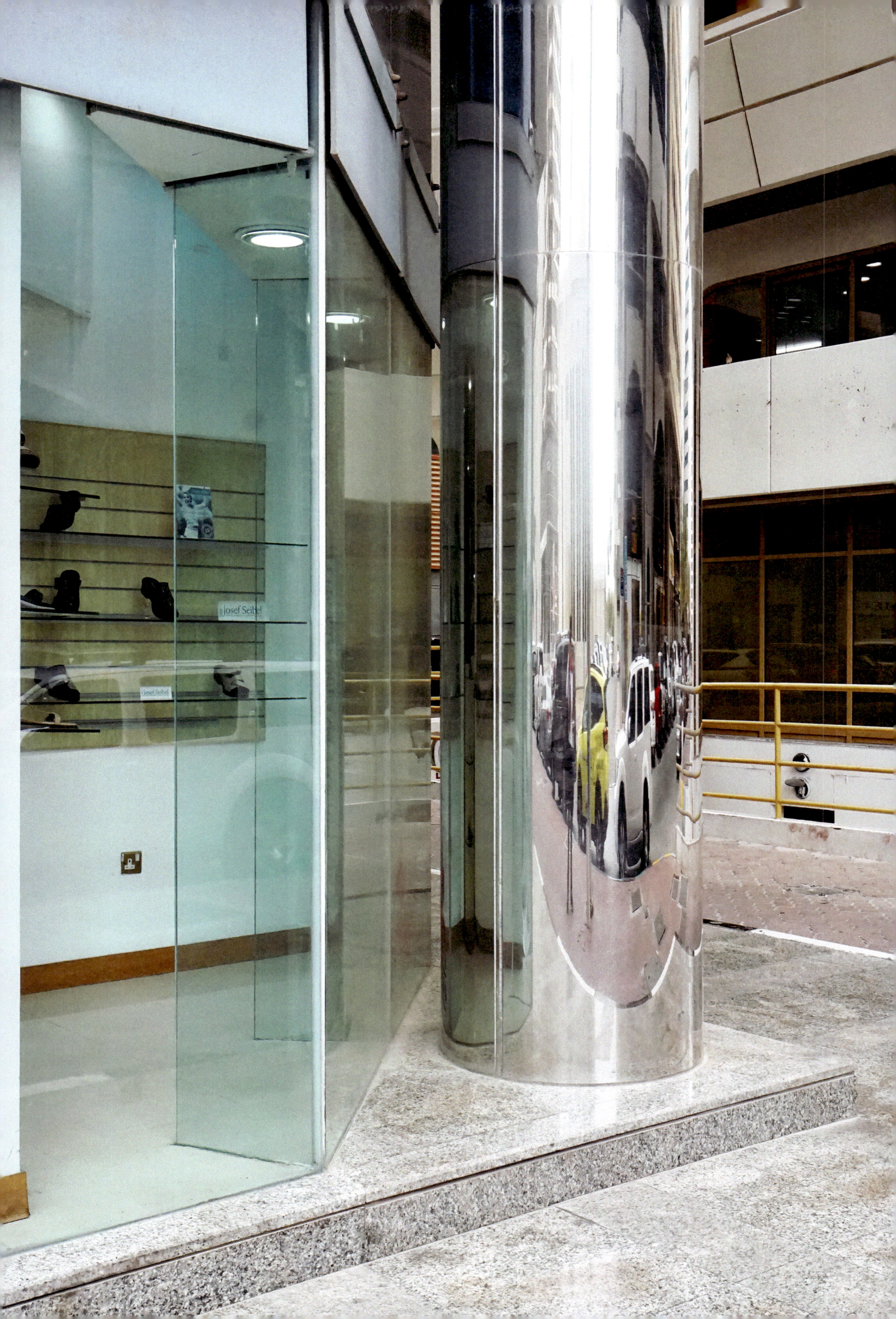

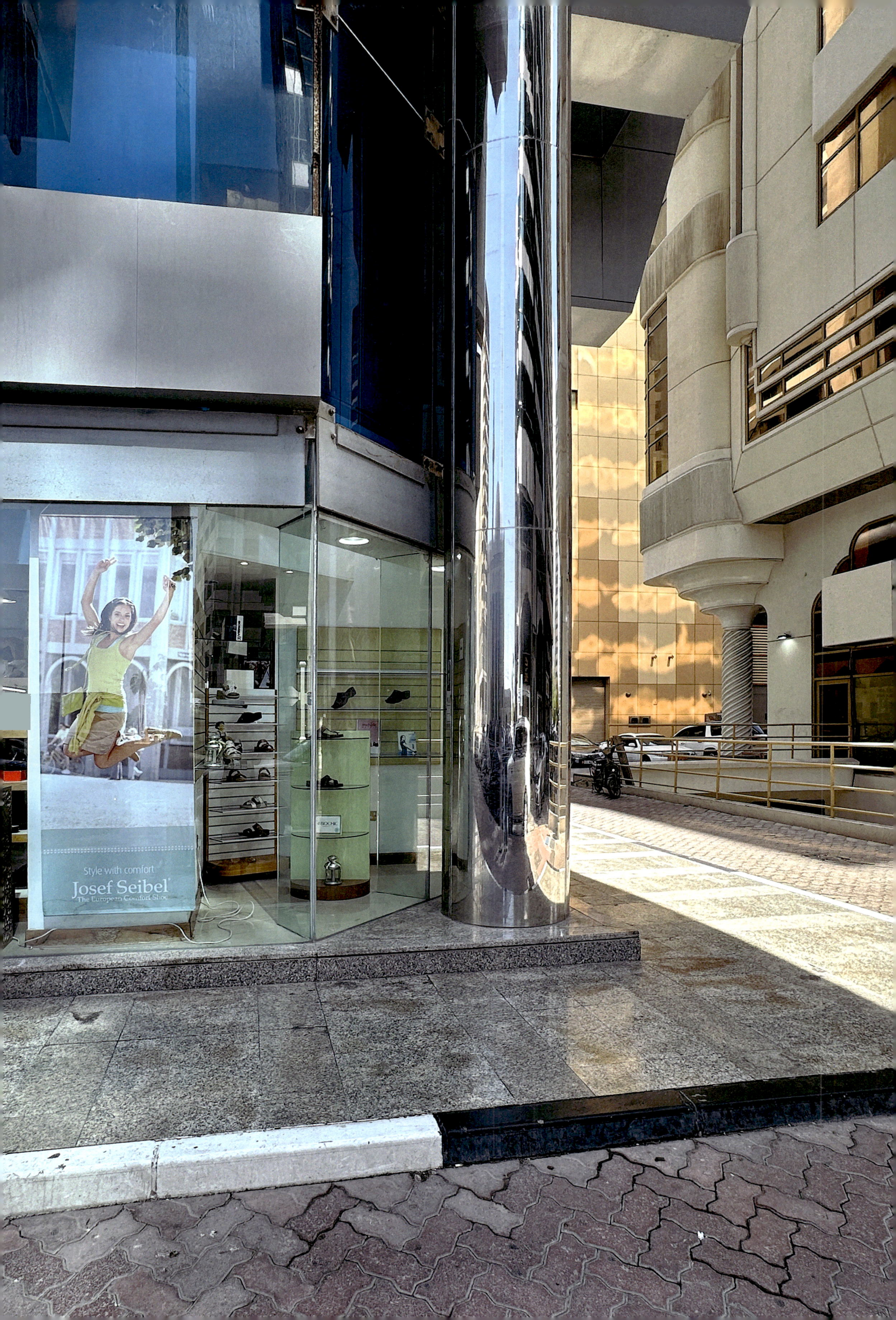

Style with comfort
Josef Seibel
The European Comfort Shoe

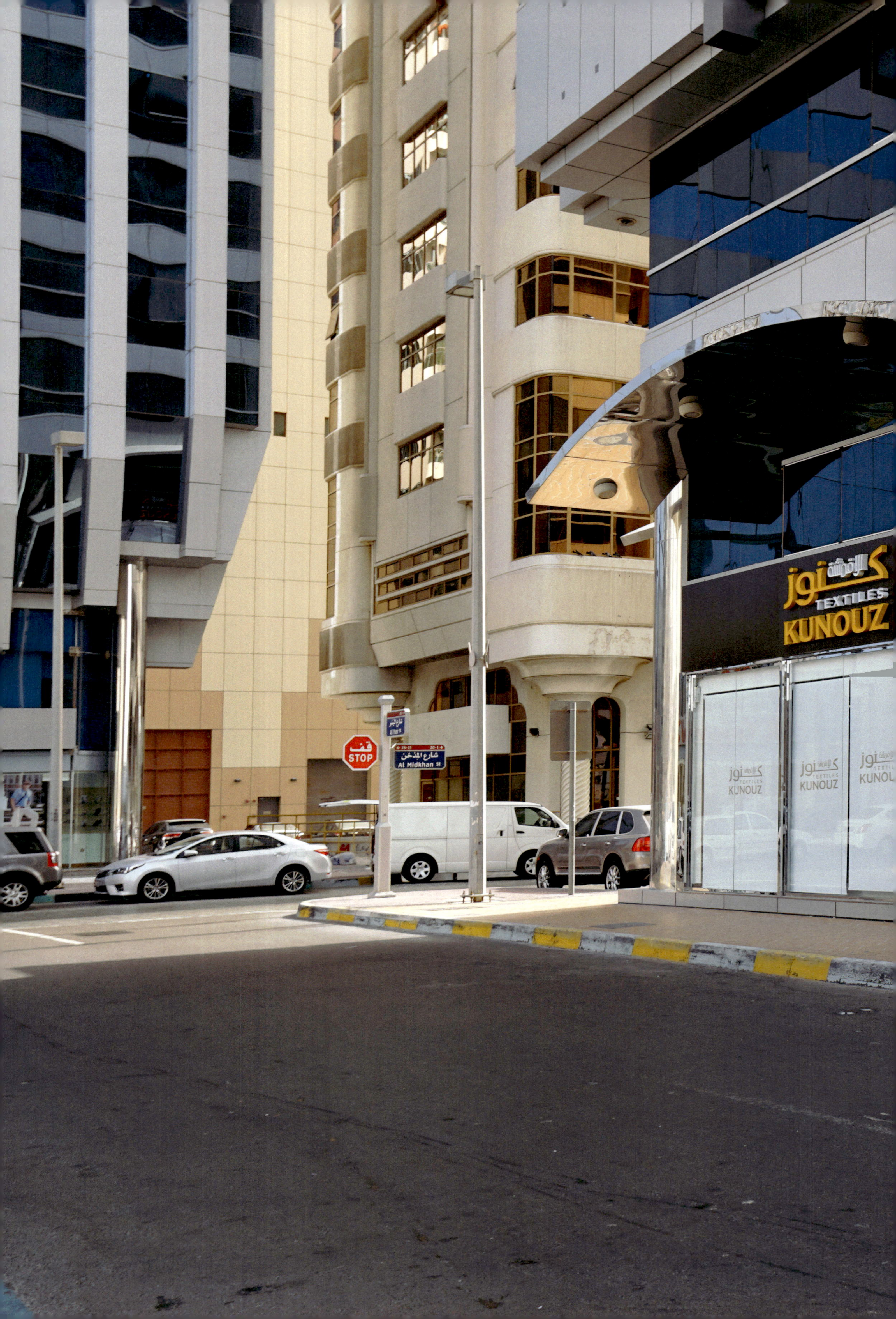
كنوز الأقمشة
TEXTILES
KUNOUZ
قف
STOP
شارع البر
Al Ber St
26-21
20-1
شارع المدخن
Al Midkhan St

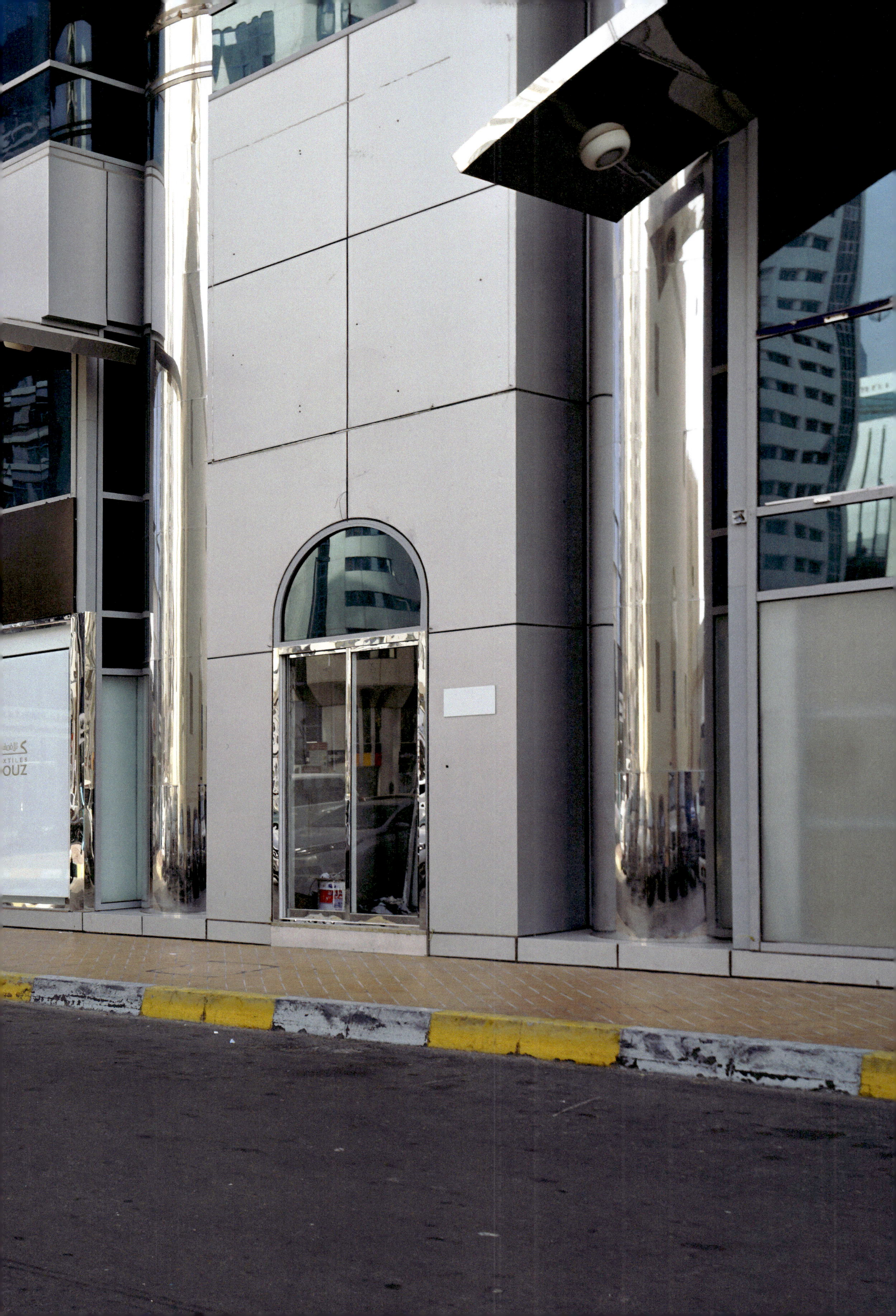

← 13
14

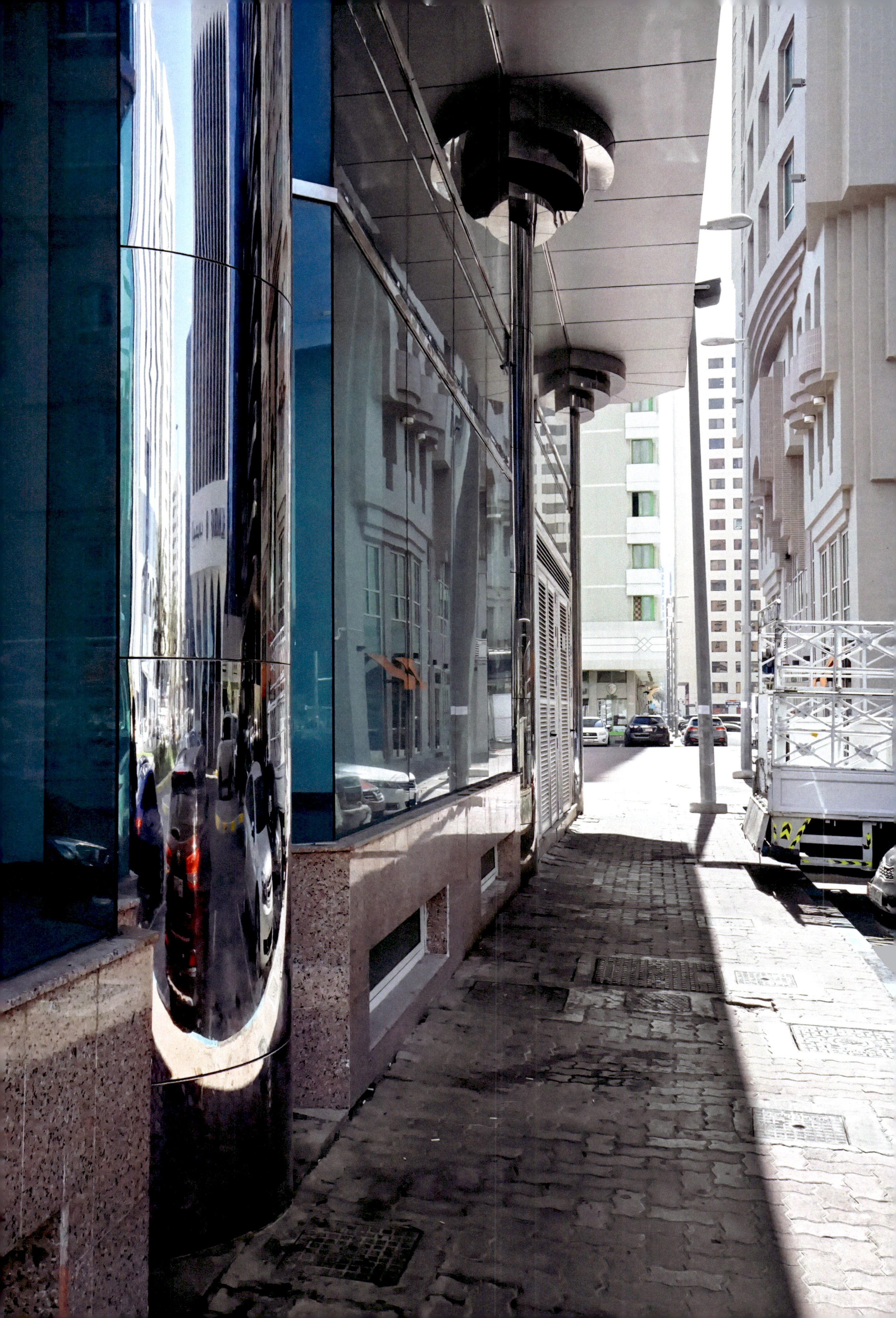

15

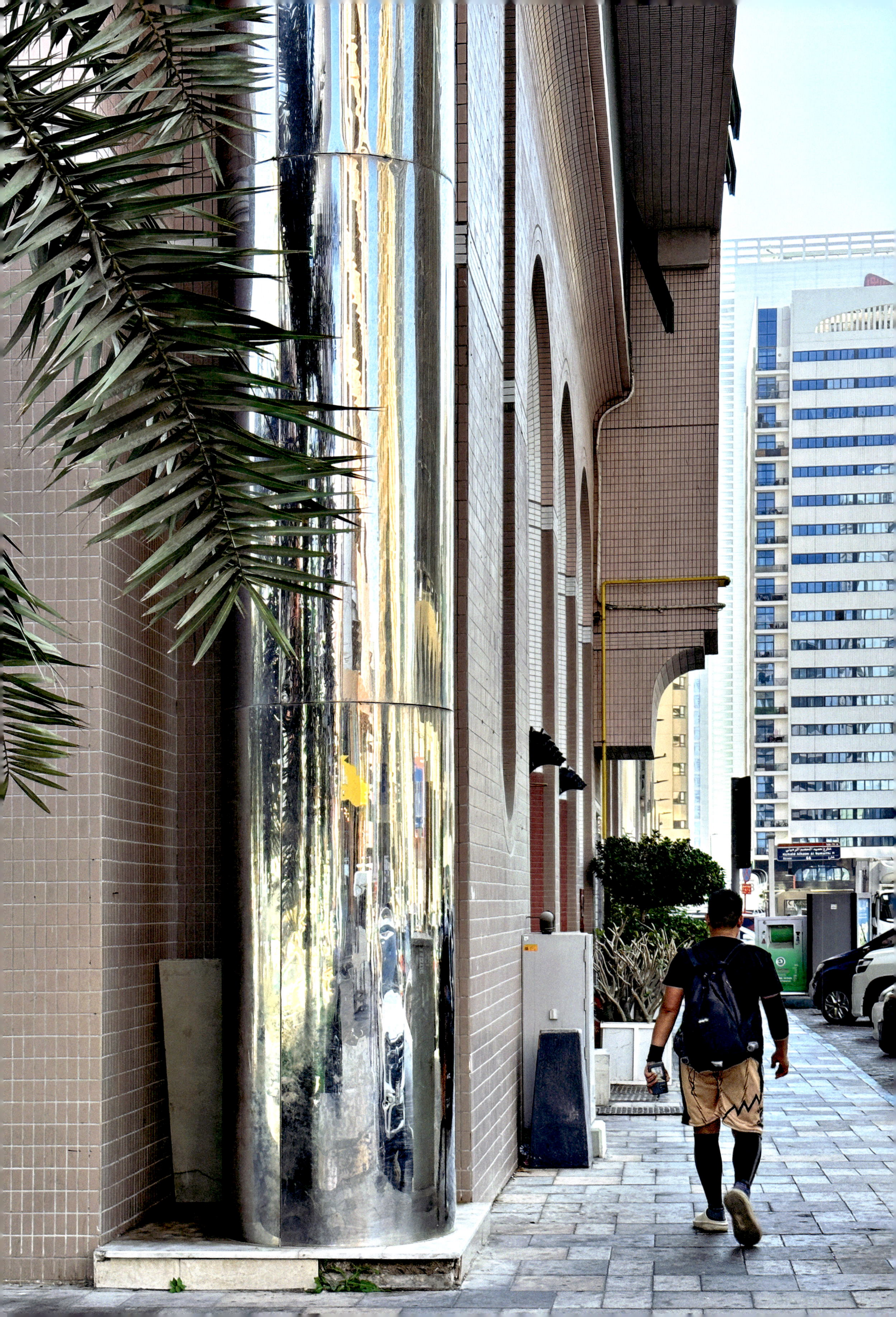

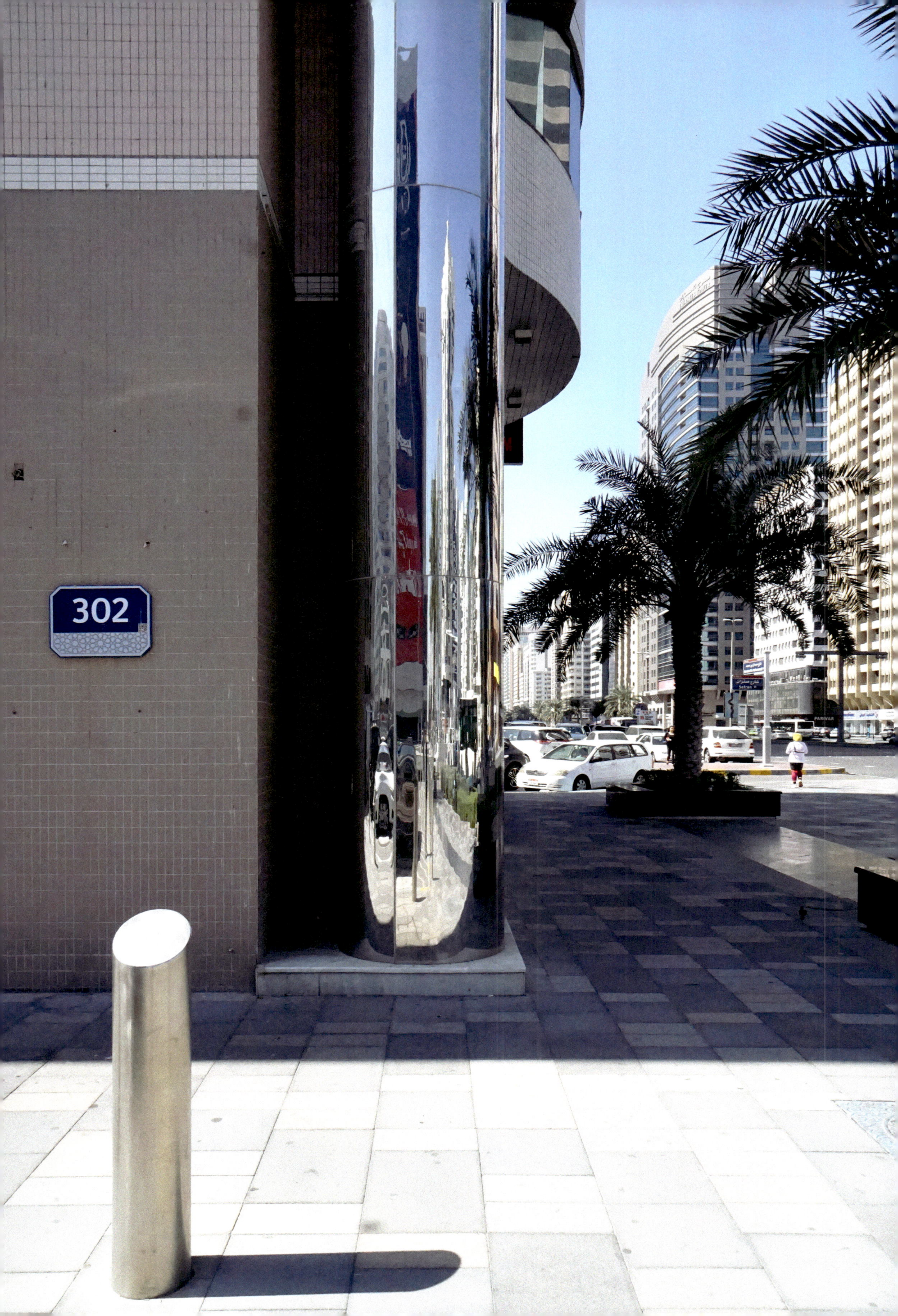
302

17

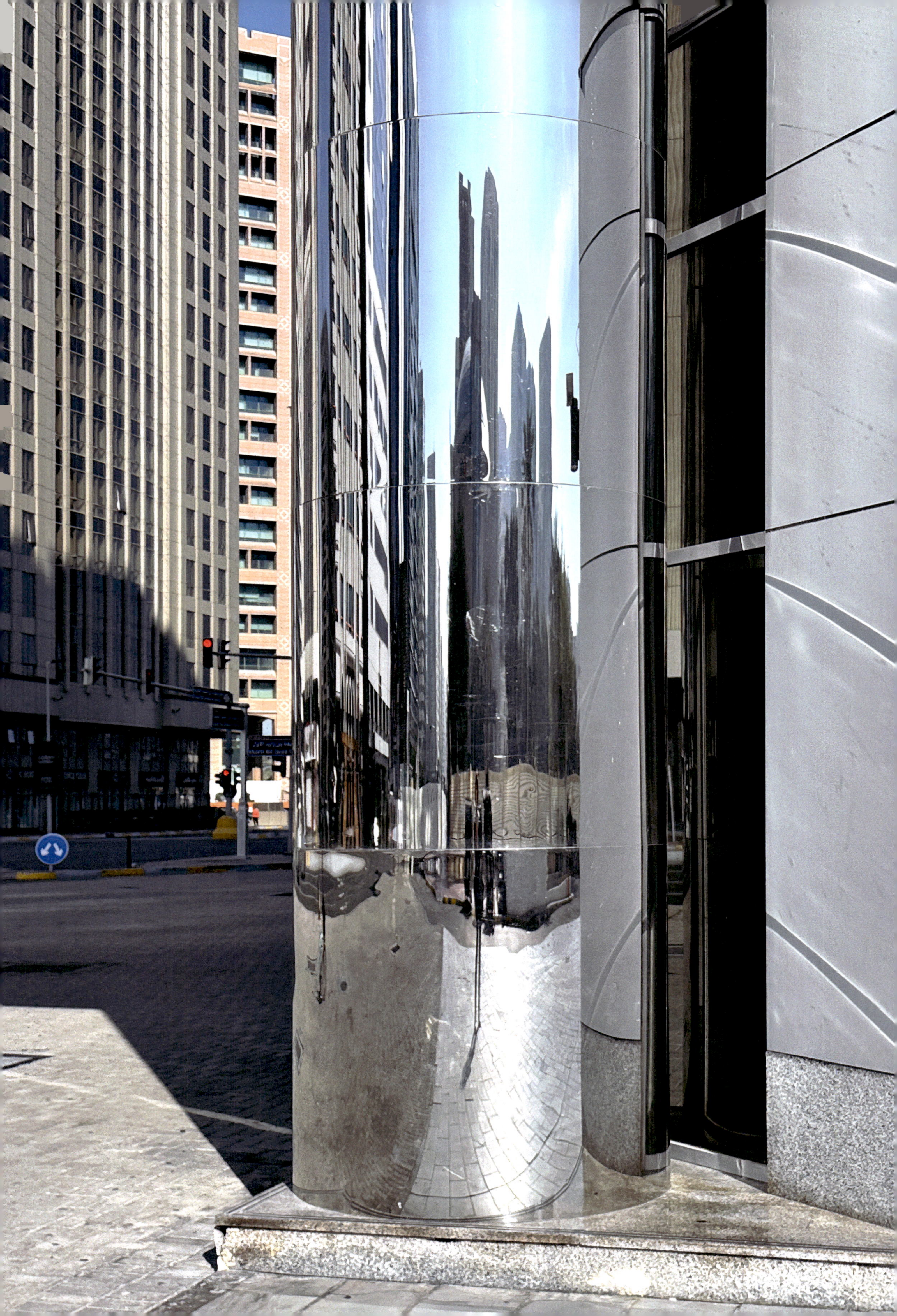

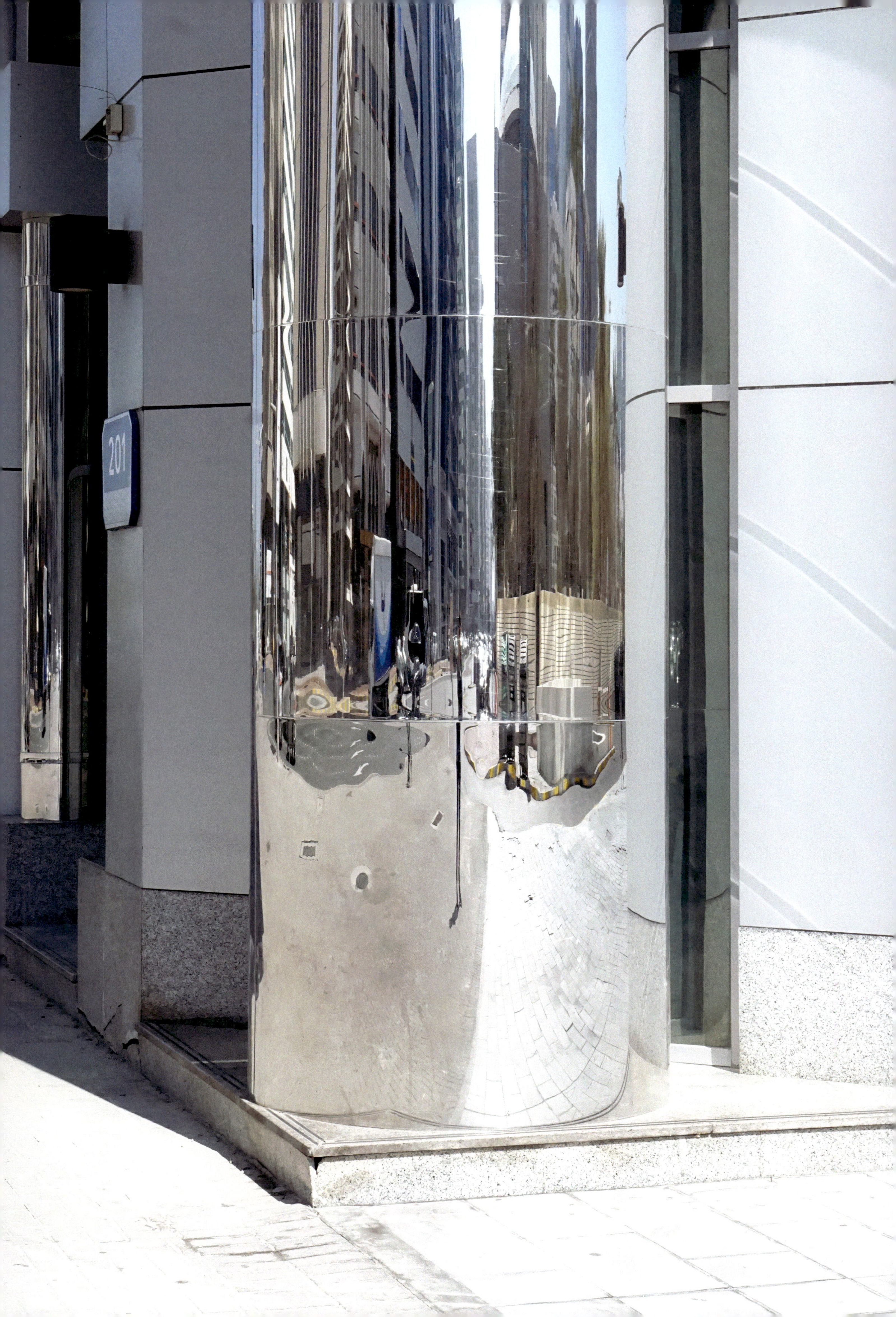

19

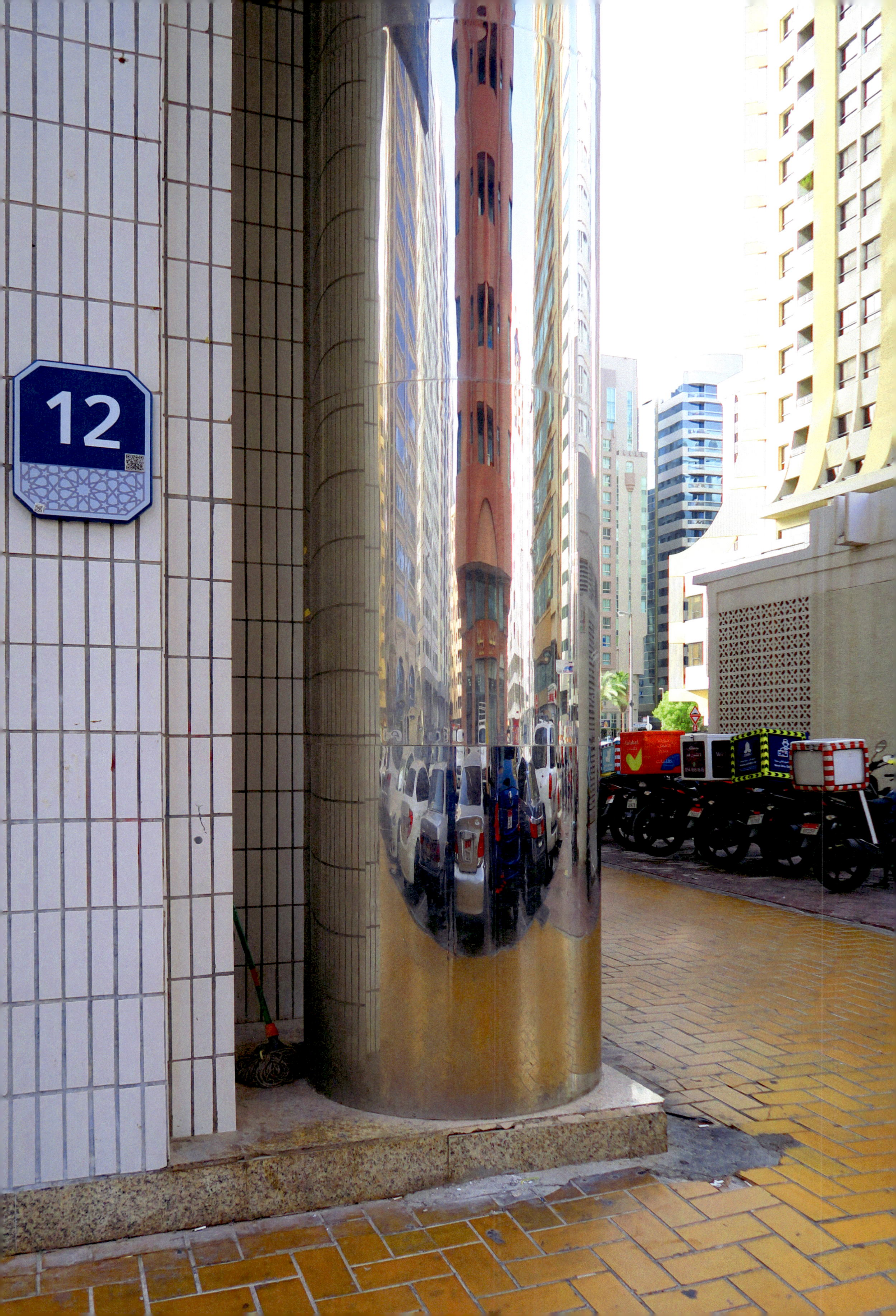

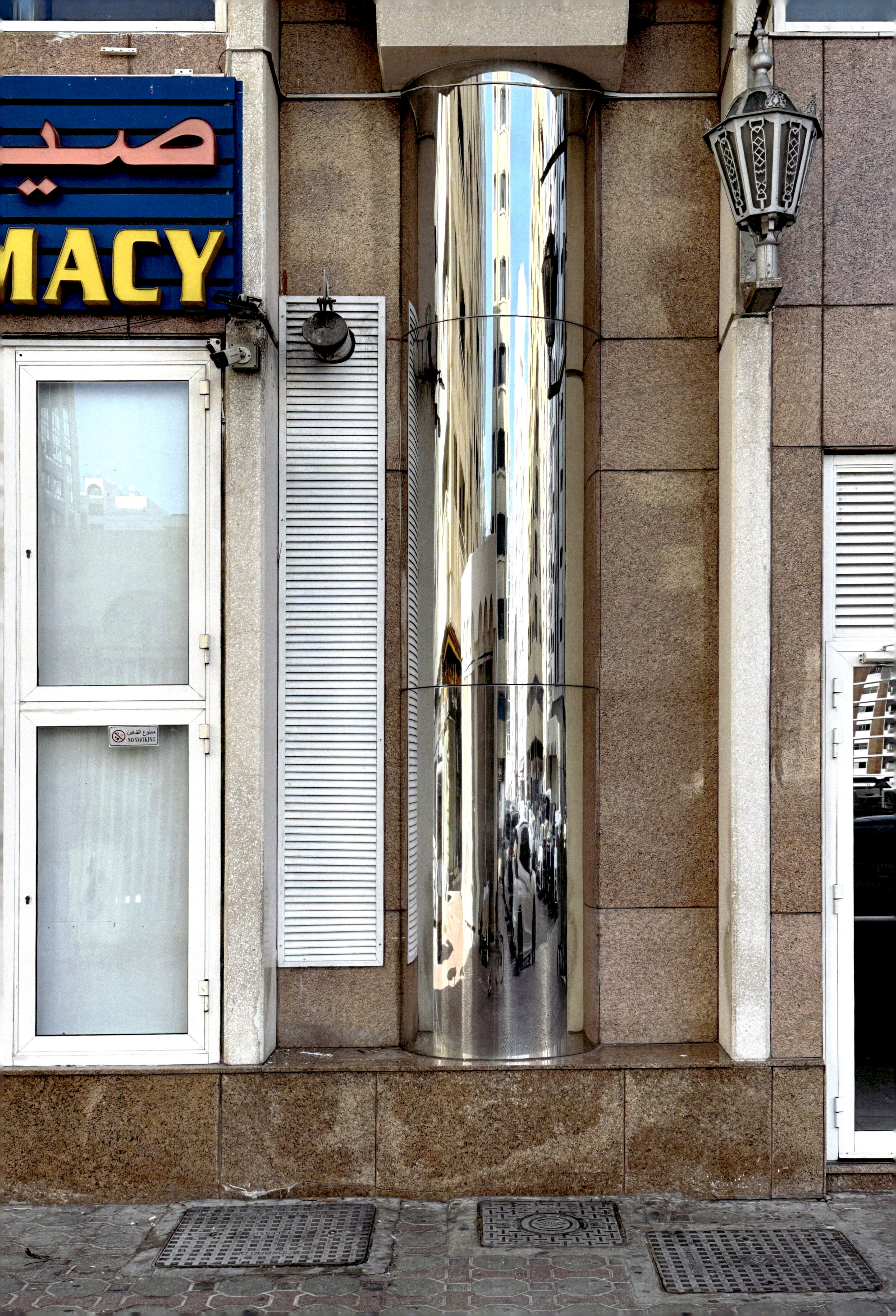
MACY
NO SMOKING

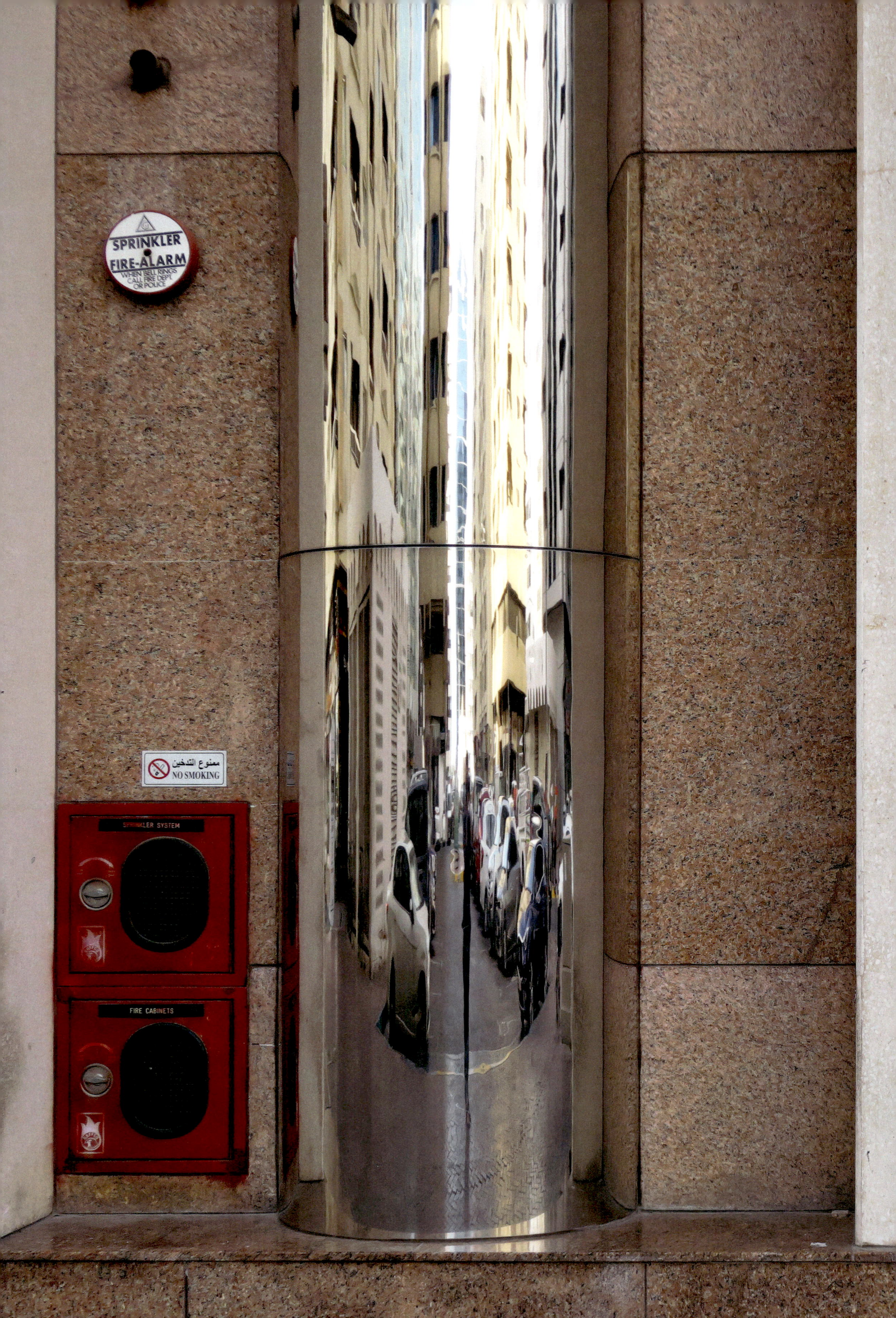
SPRINKLER
FIRE-ALARM
WHEN BELL RINGS
CALL FIRE DEPT
OR POLICE
ممنوع التدخين
NO SMOKING
SPRINKLER SYSTEM
FIRE CABINETS

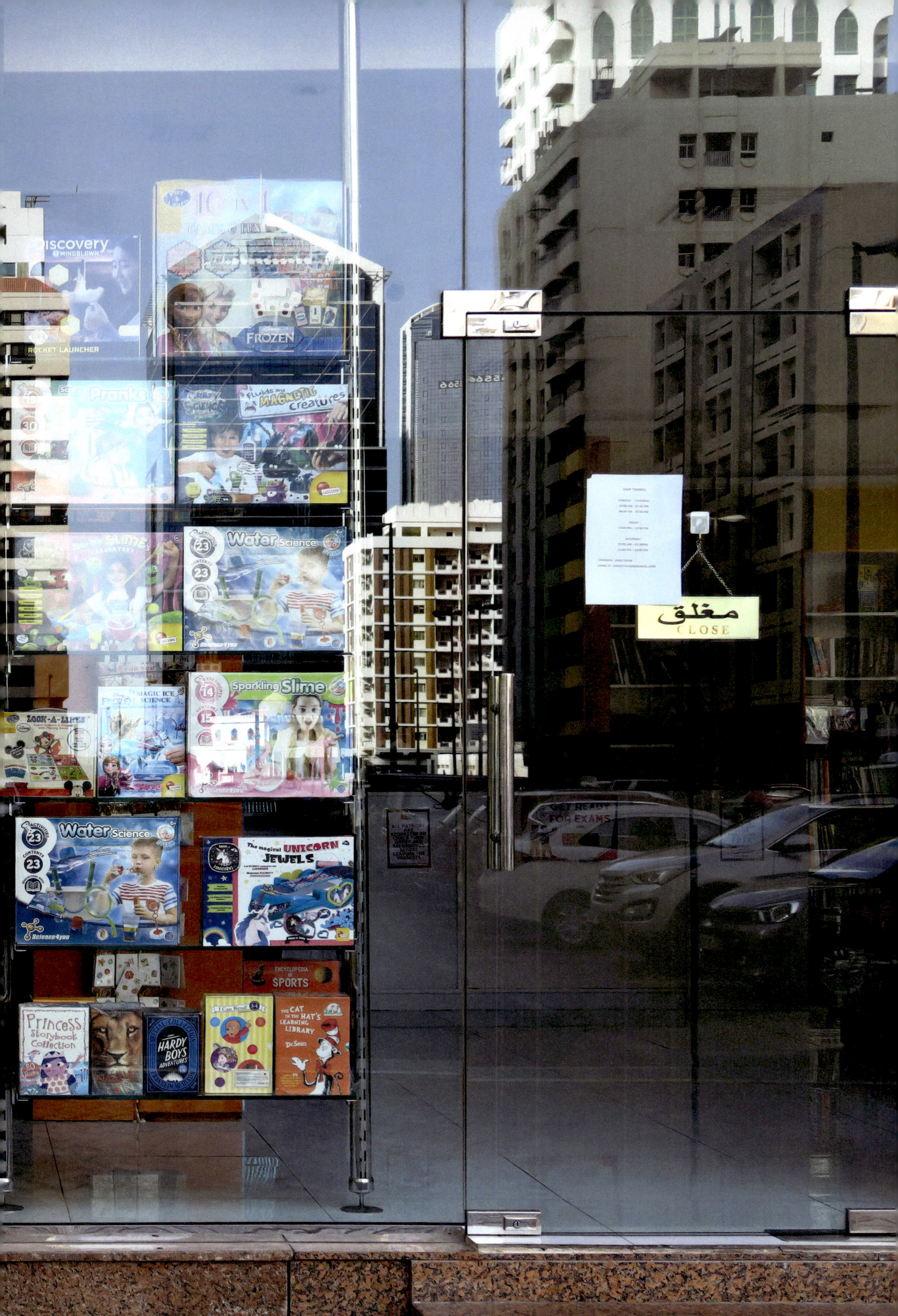
معلق
CLOSE

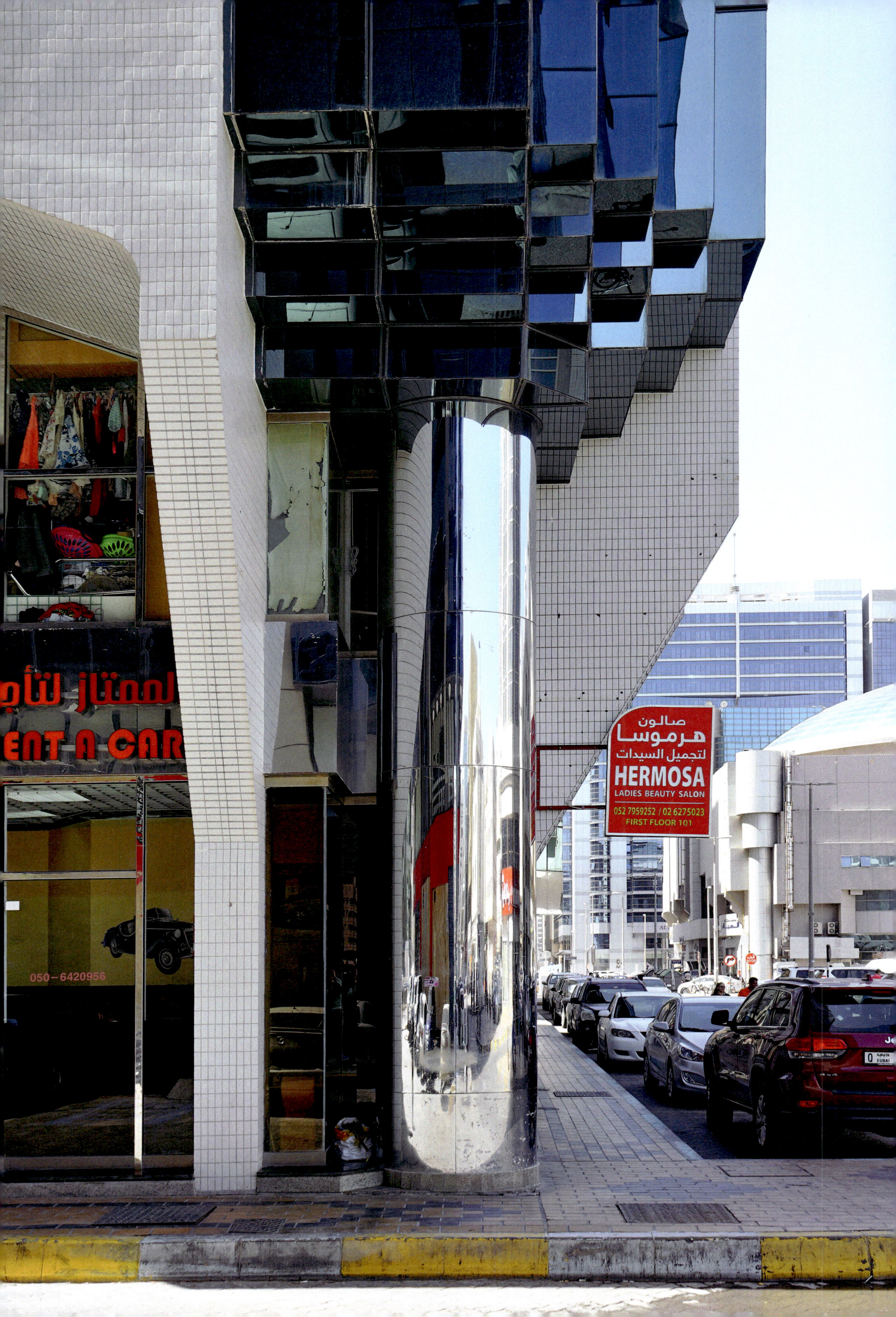
ENT A CAR
050-6420956
صالون
هرموسا
لتجميل السيدات
HERMOSA
LADIES BEAUTY SALON
052 7959252 / 02 6275023
FIRST FLOOR 101

23

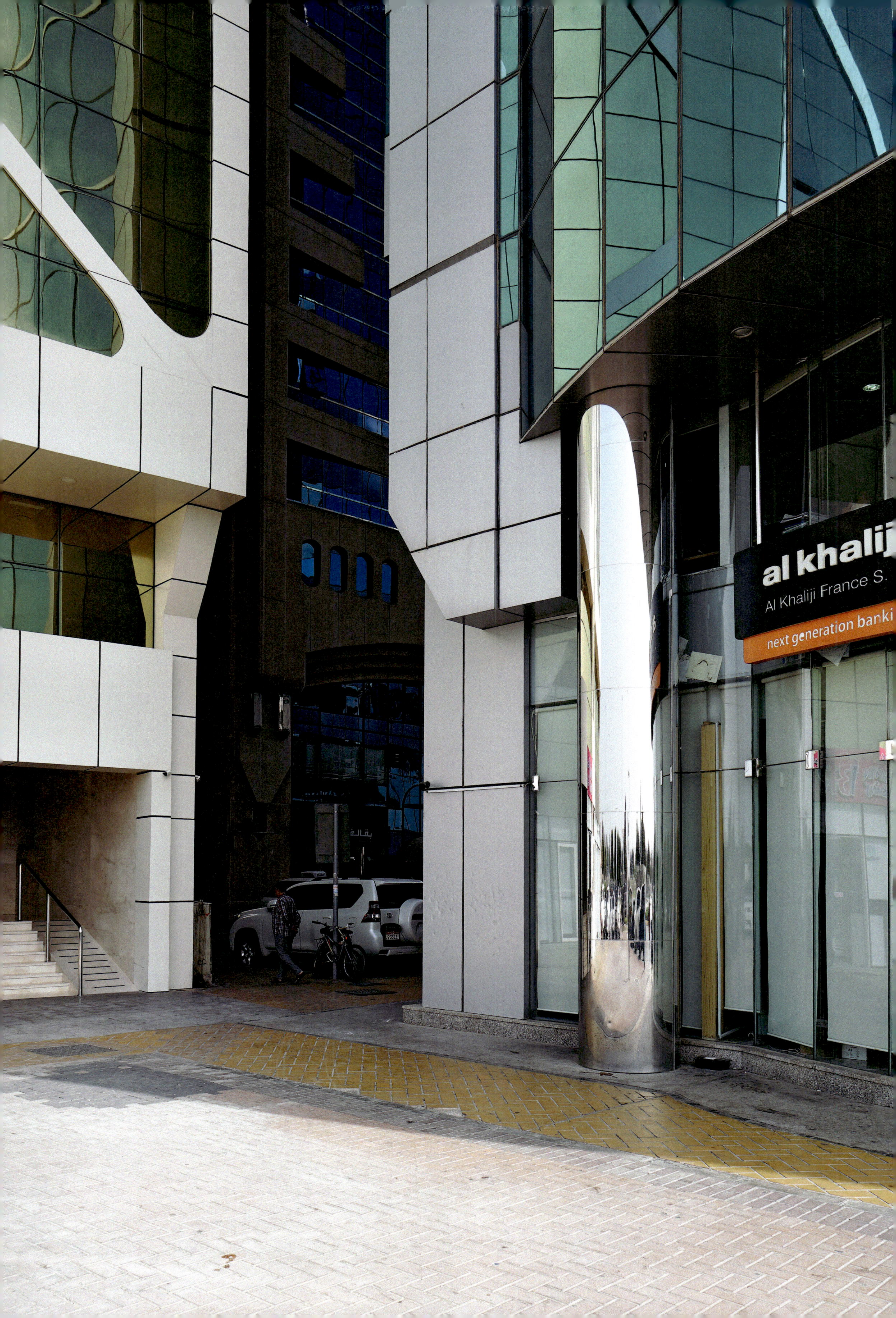
al khalij
Al Khaliji France S.
next generation banki

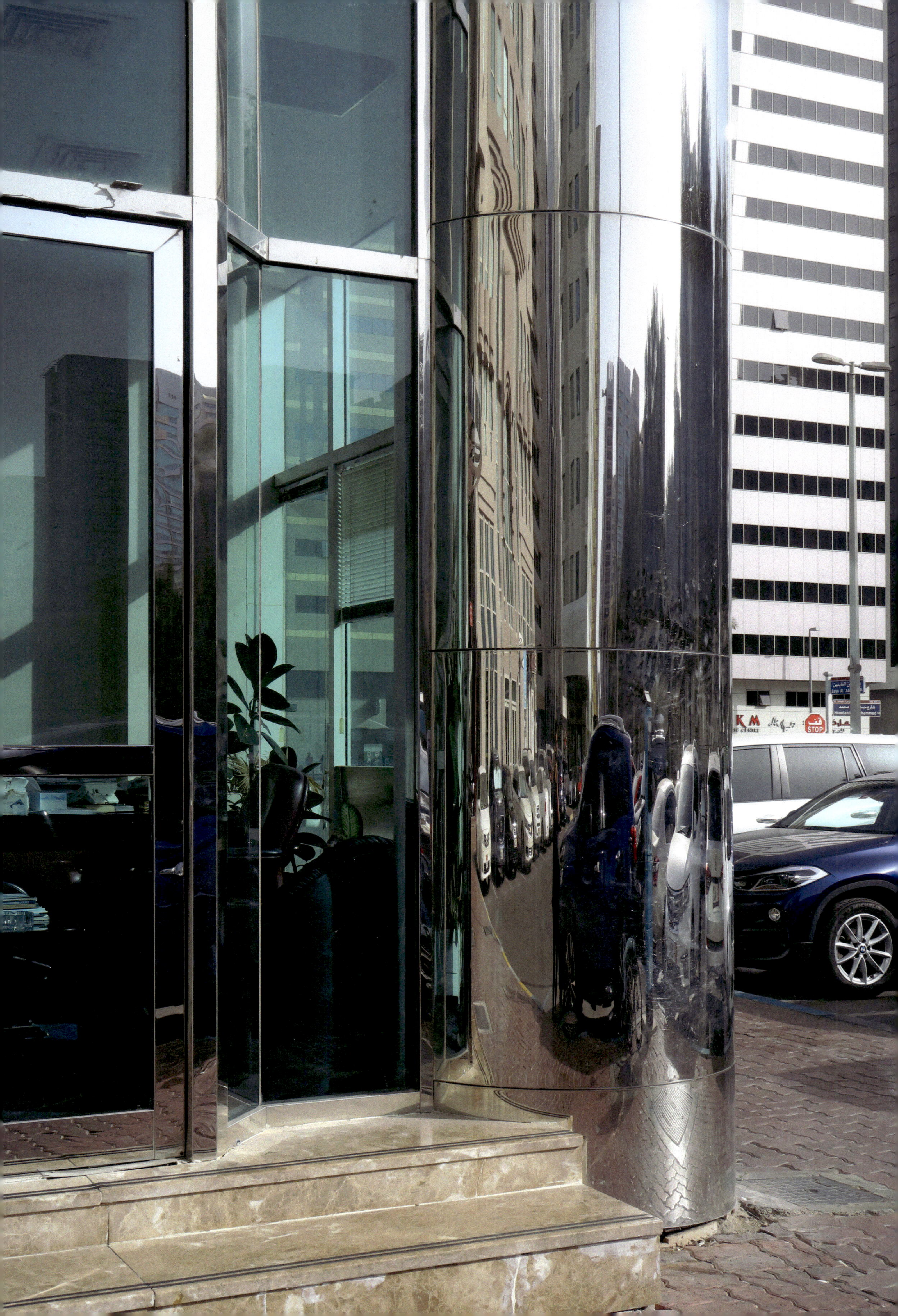

25

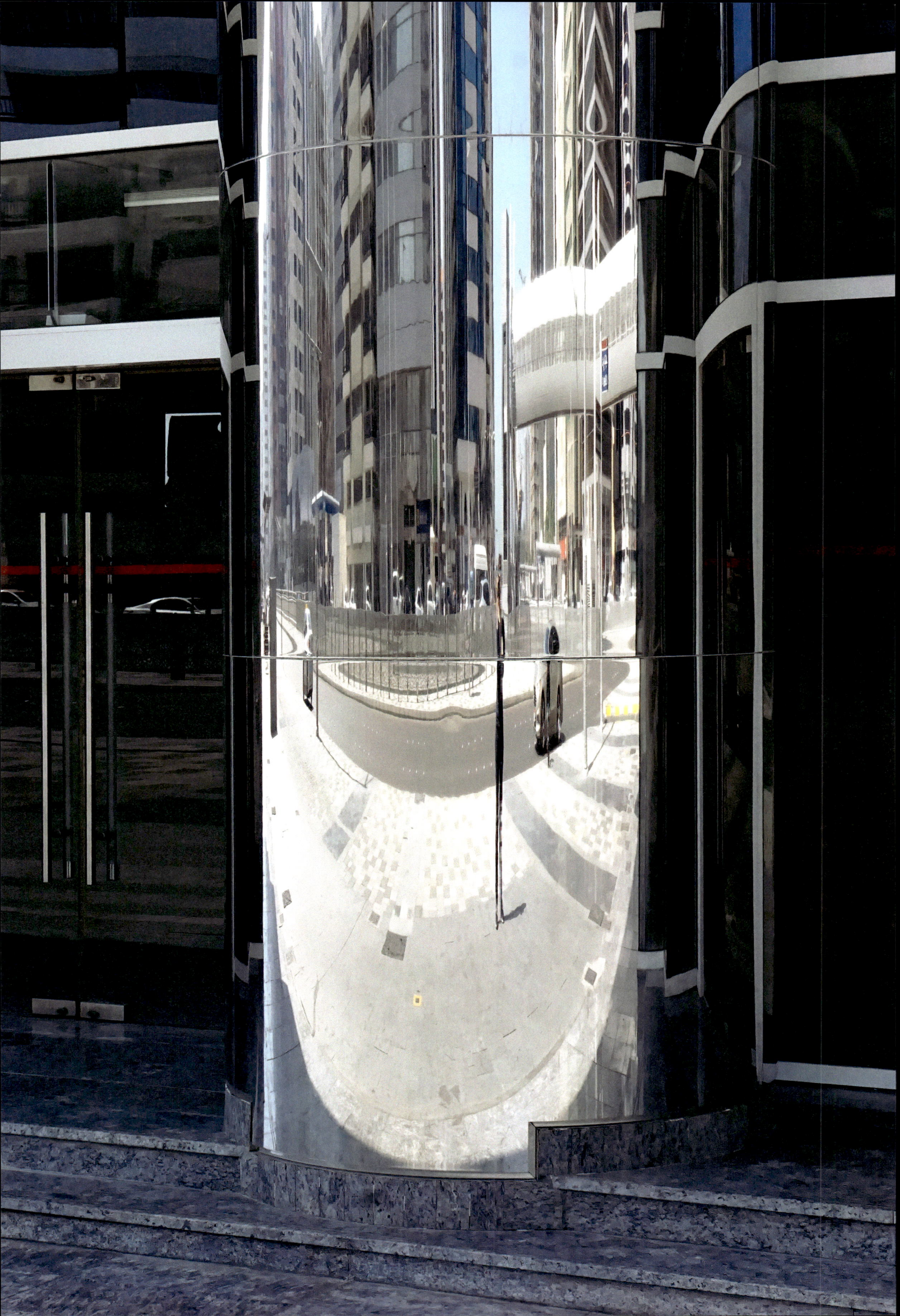

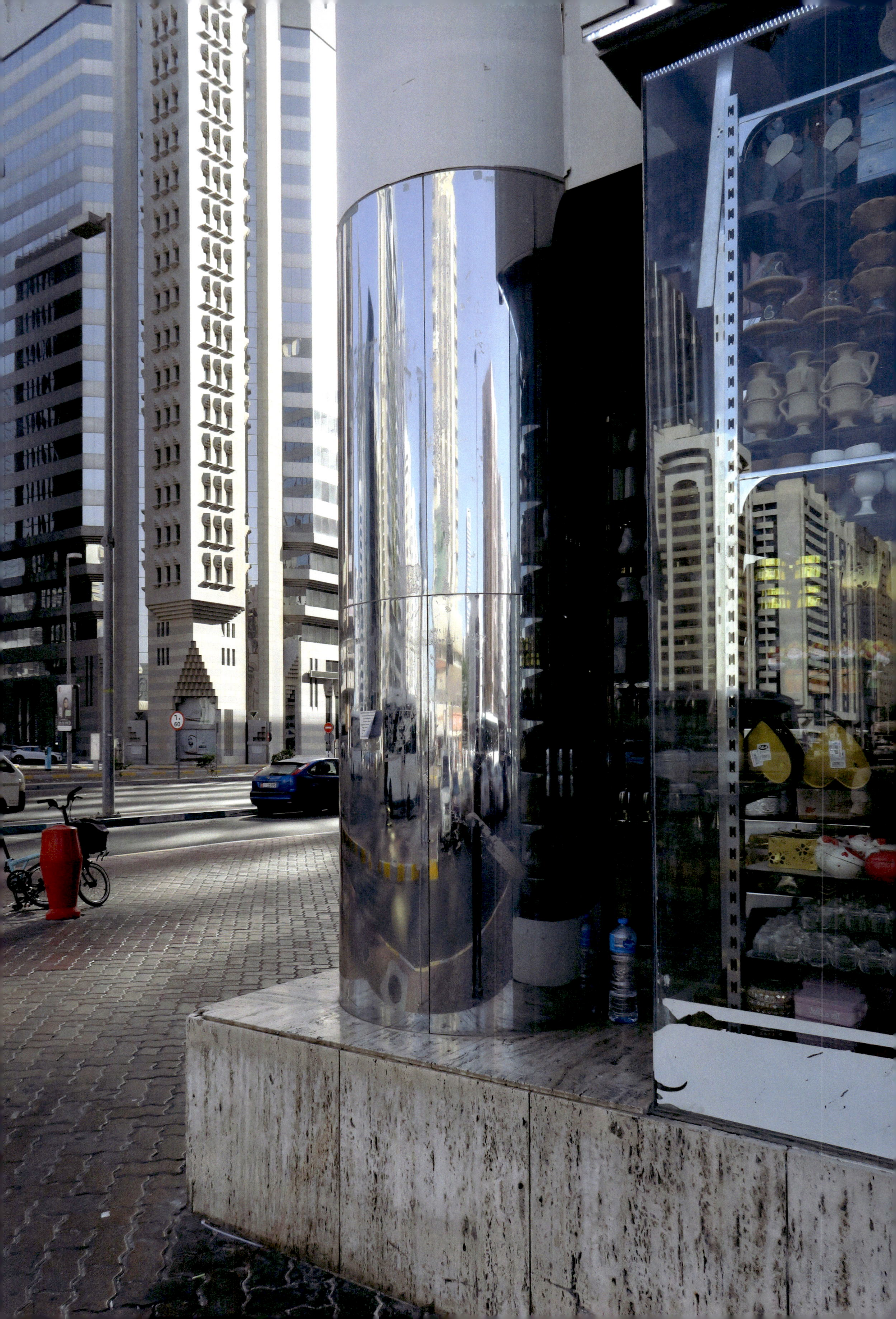

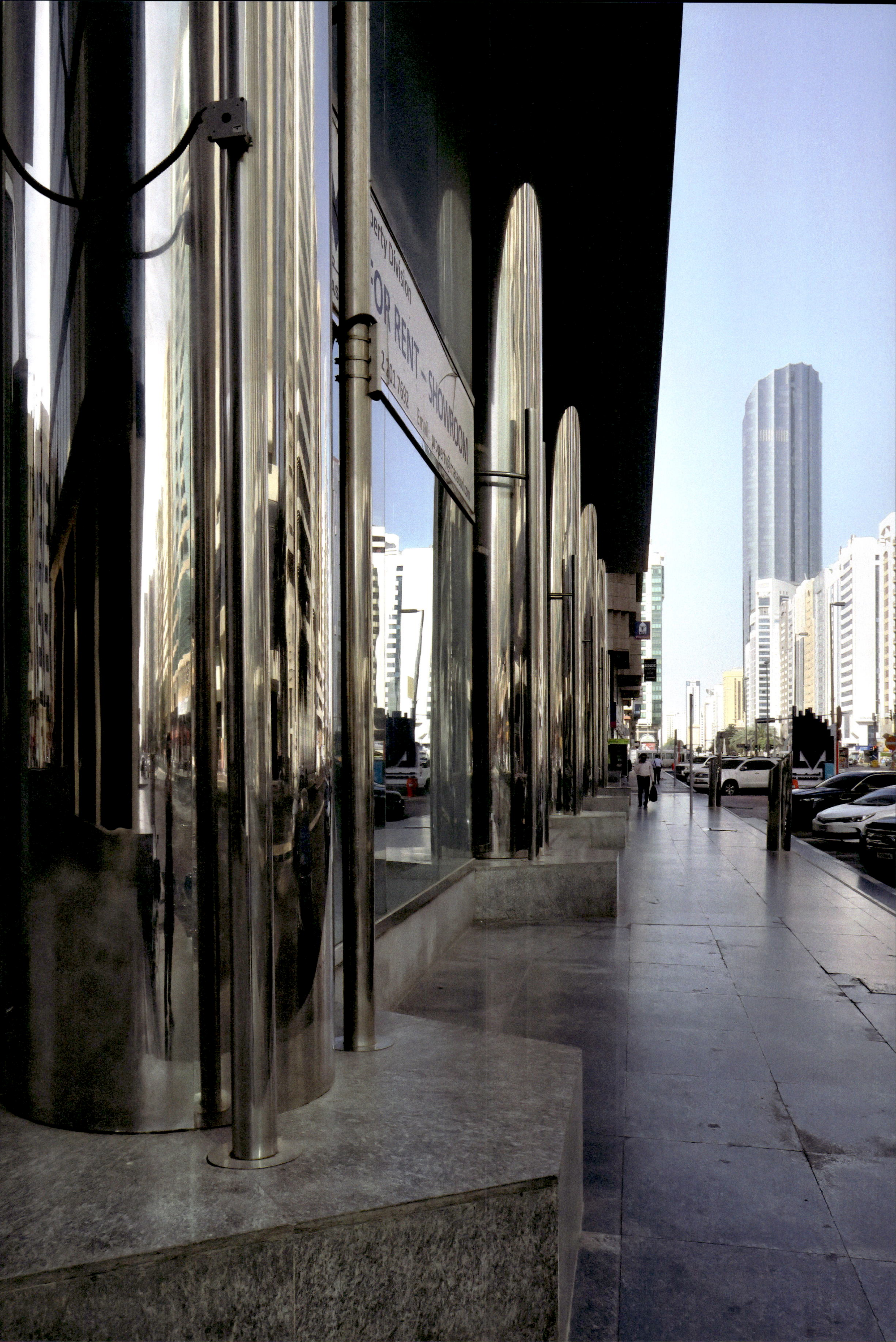

perty Division
FOR RENT - SHOWROOM
2 401 7692
Email: property@masaood.com

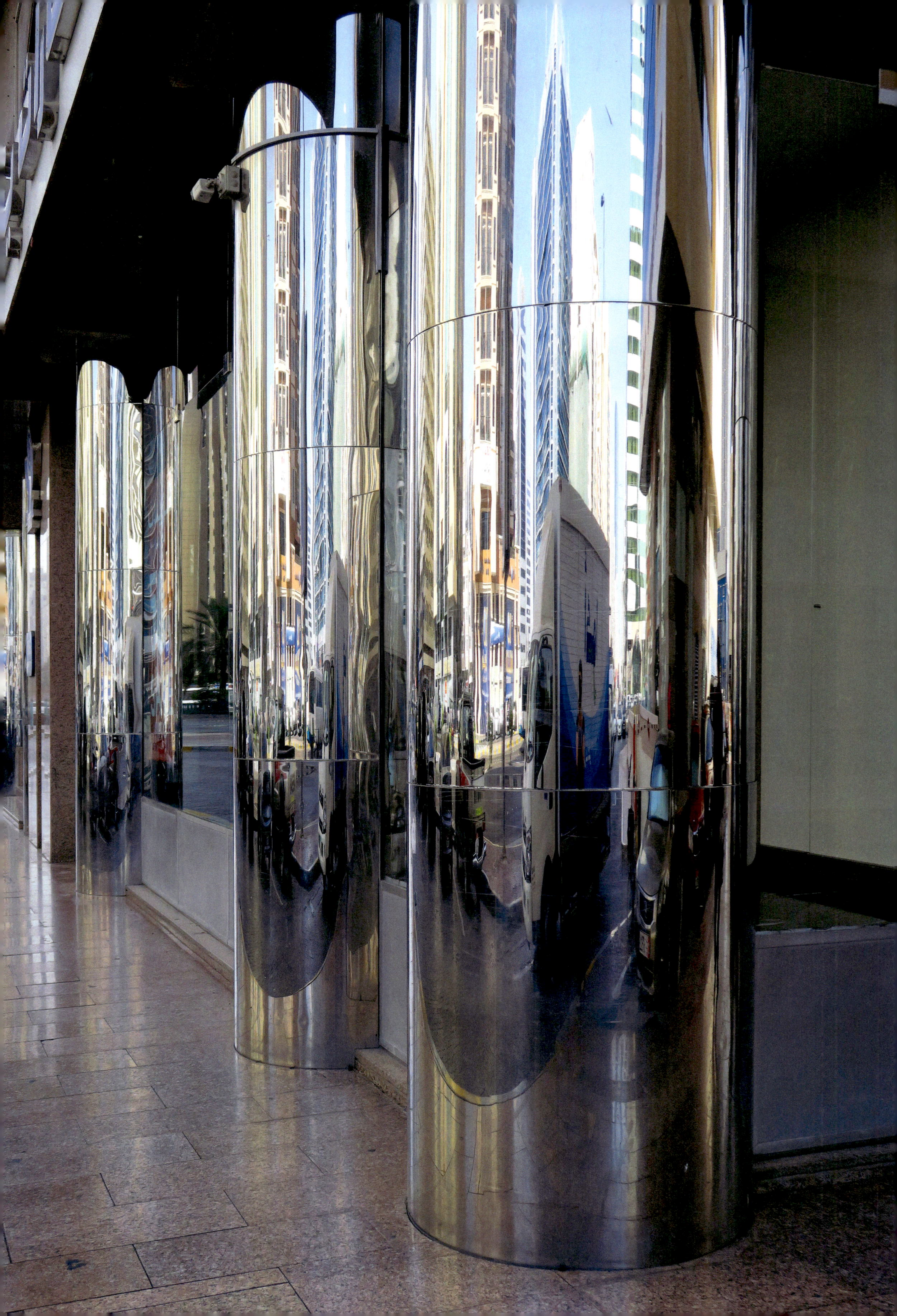

29

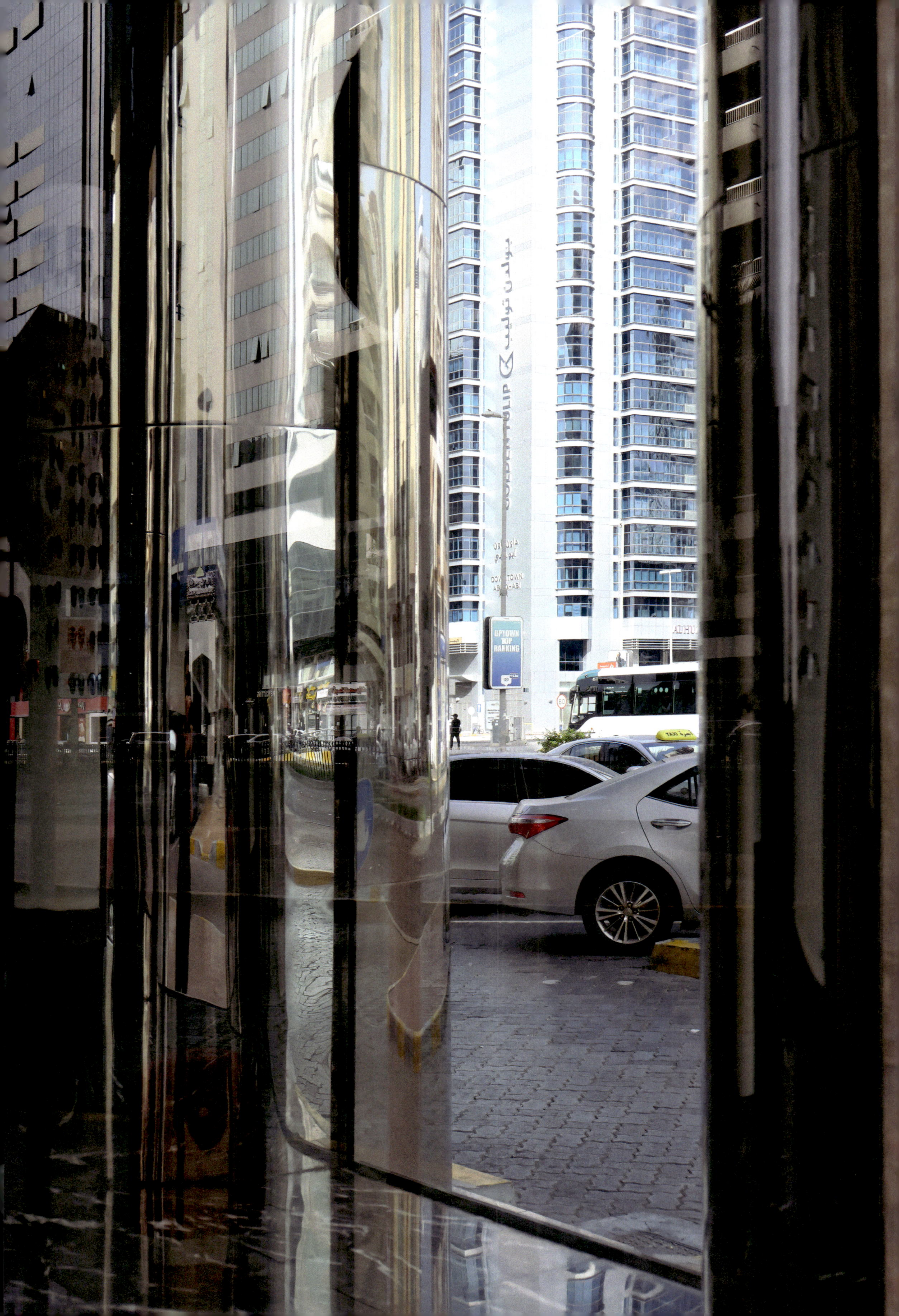

30

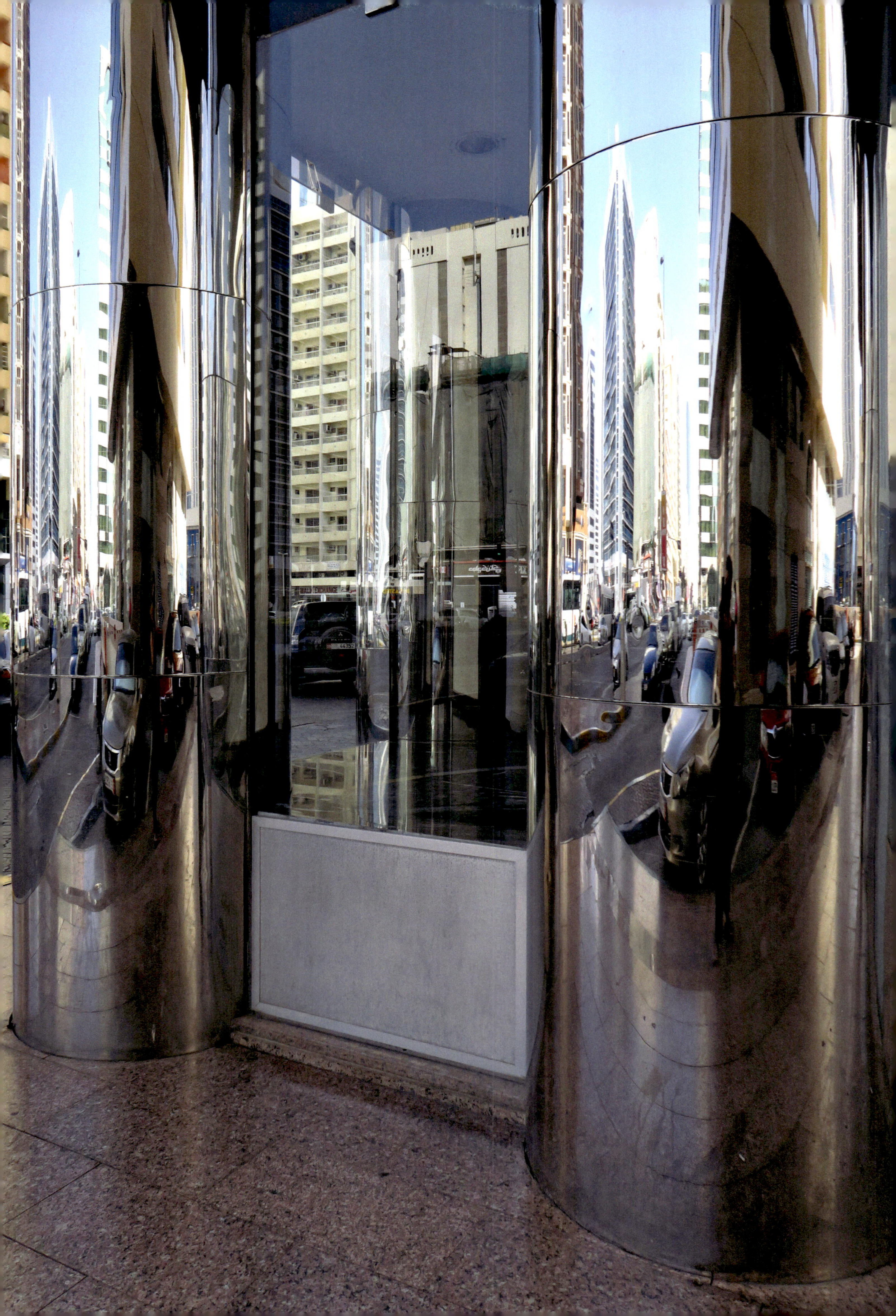

31

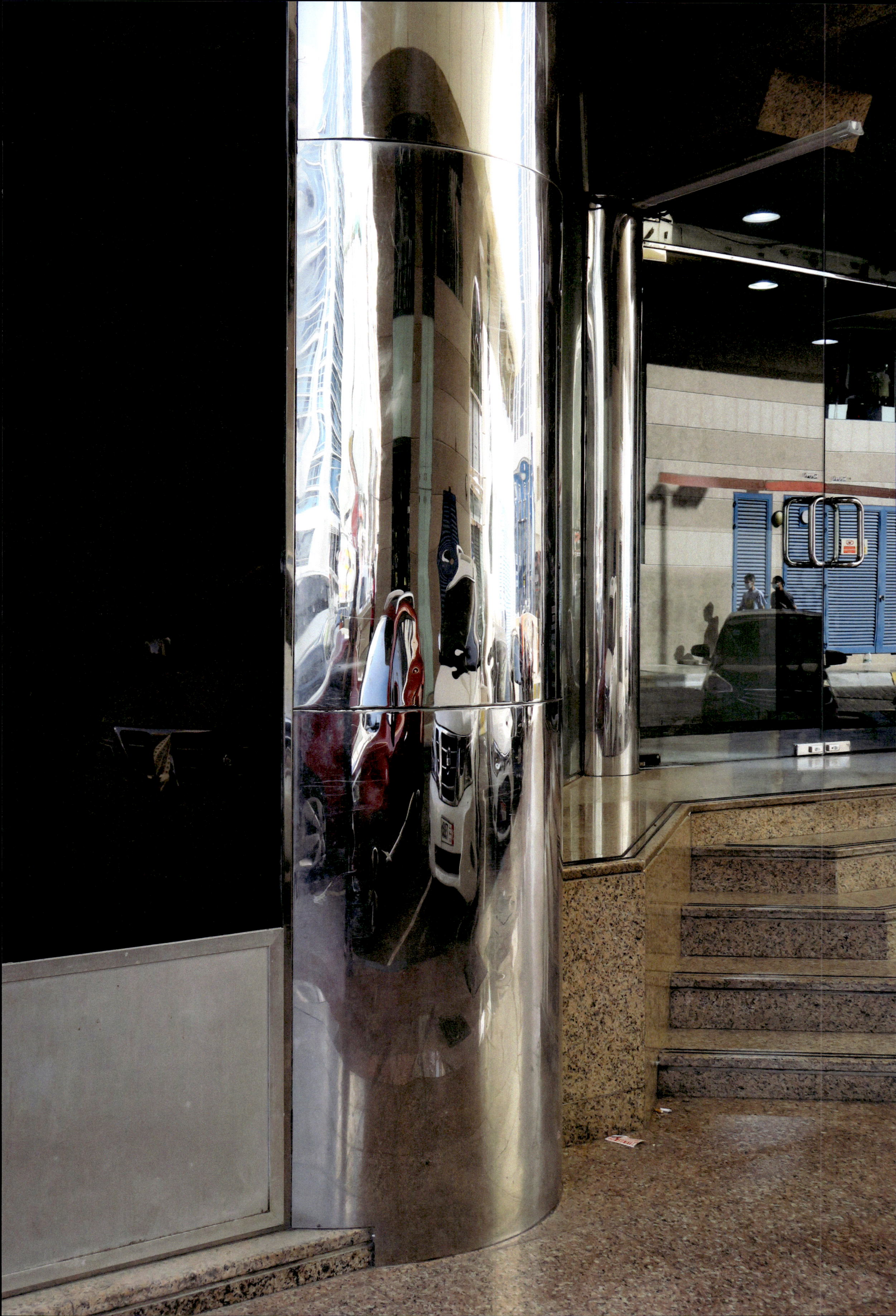

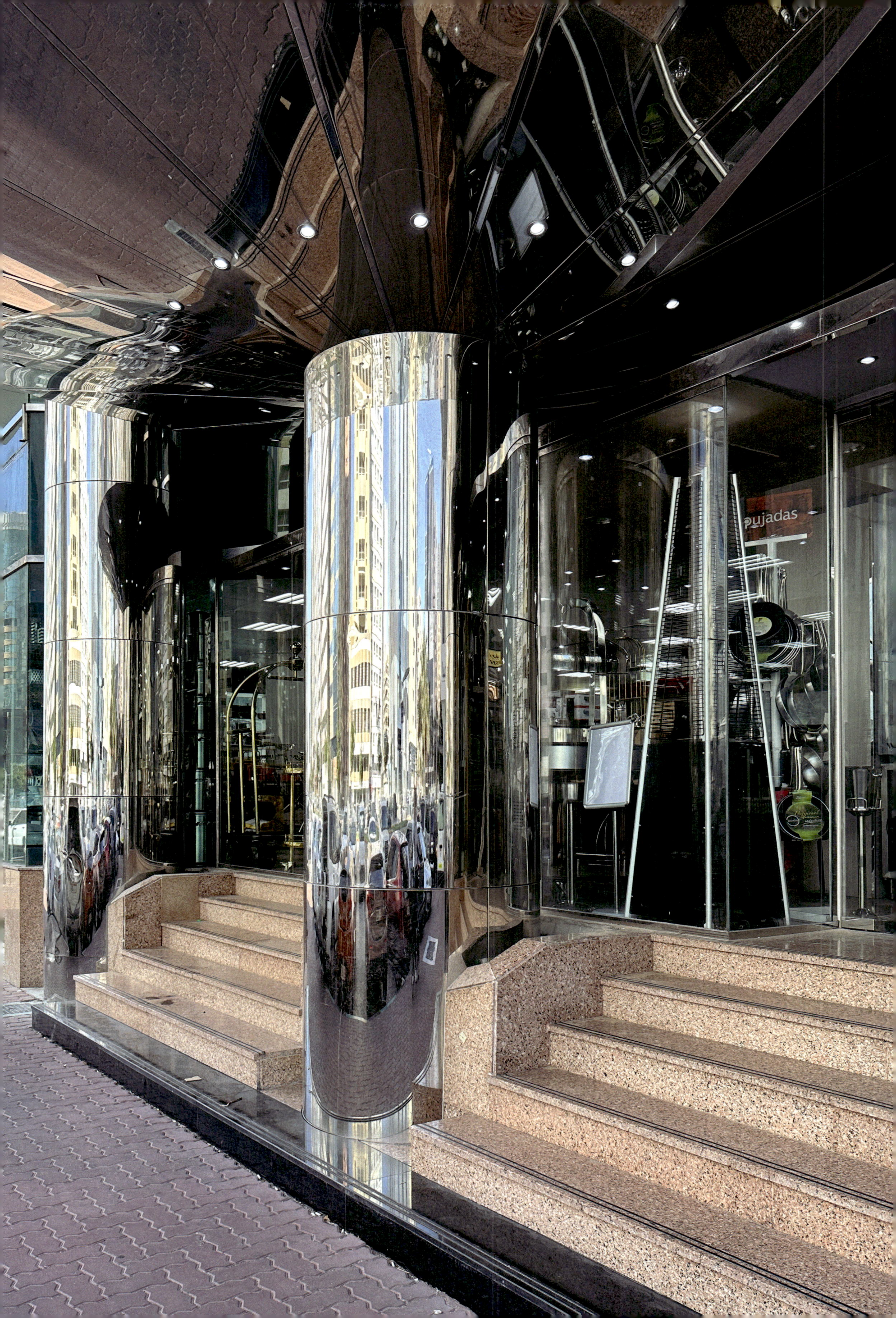

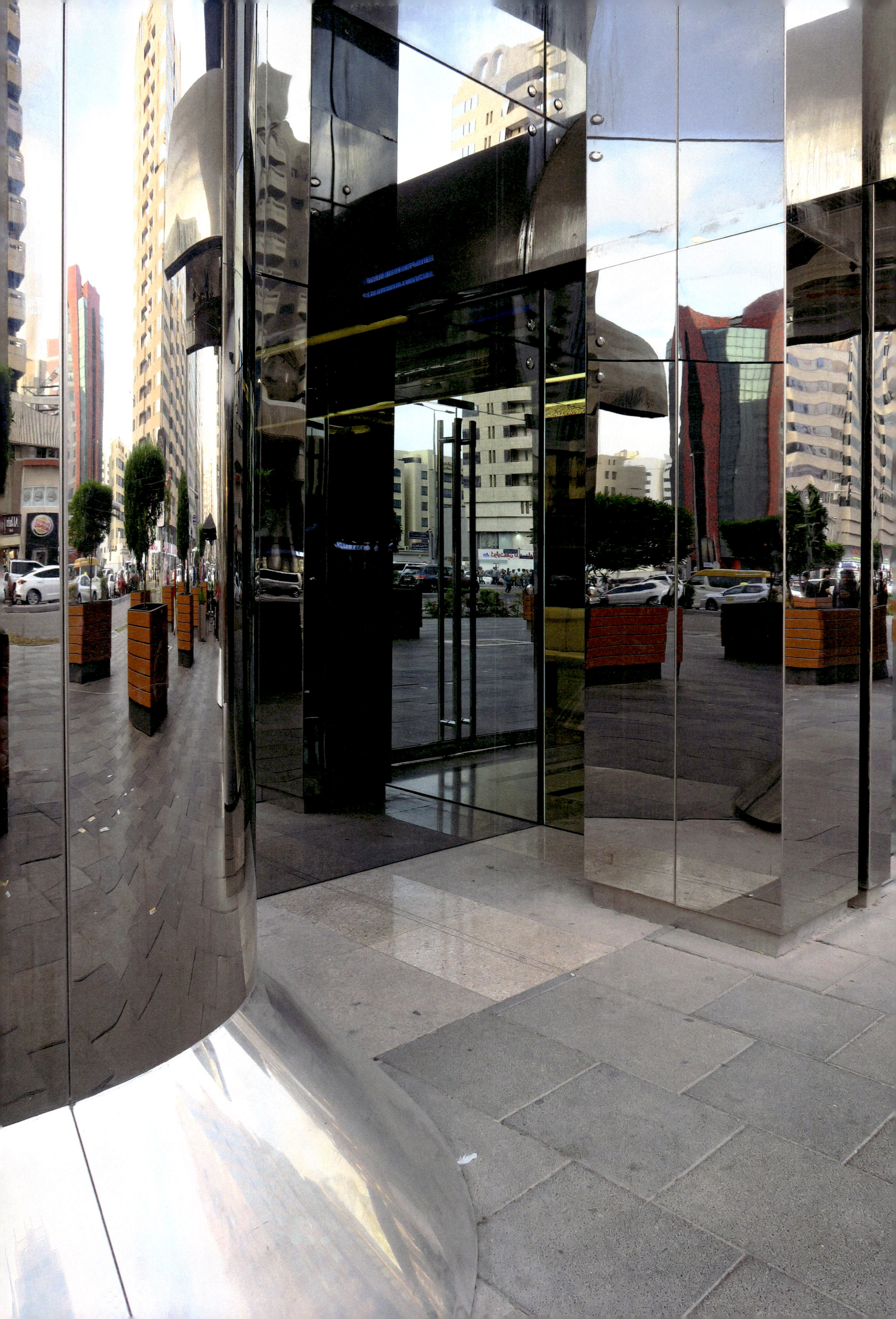

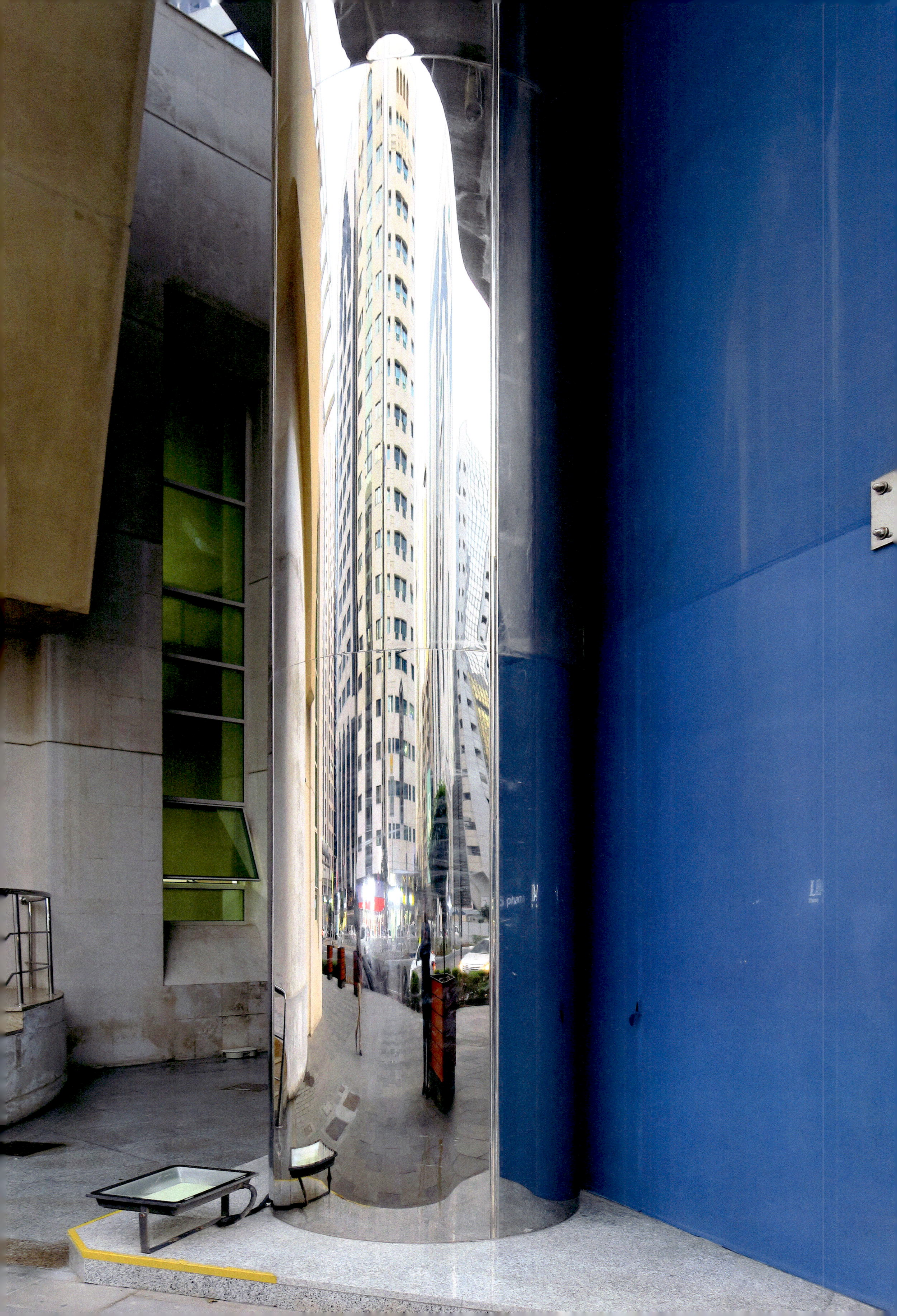

35

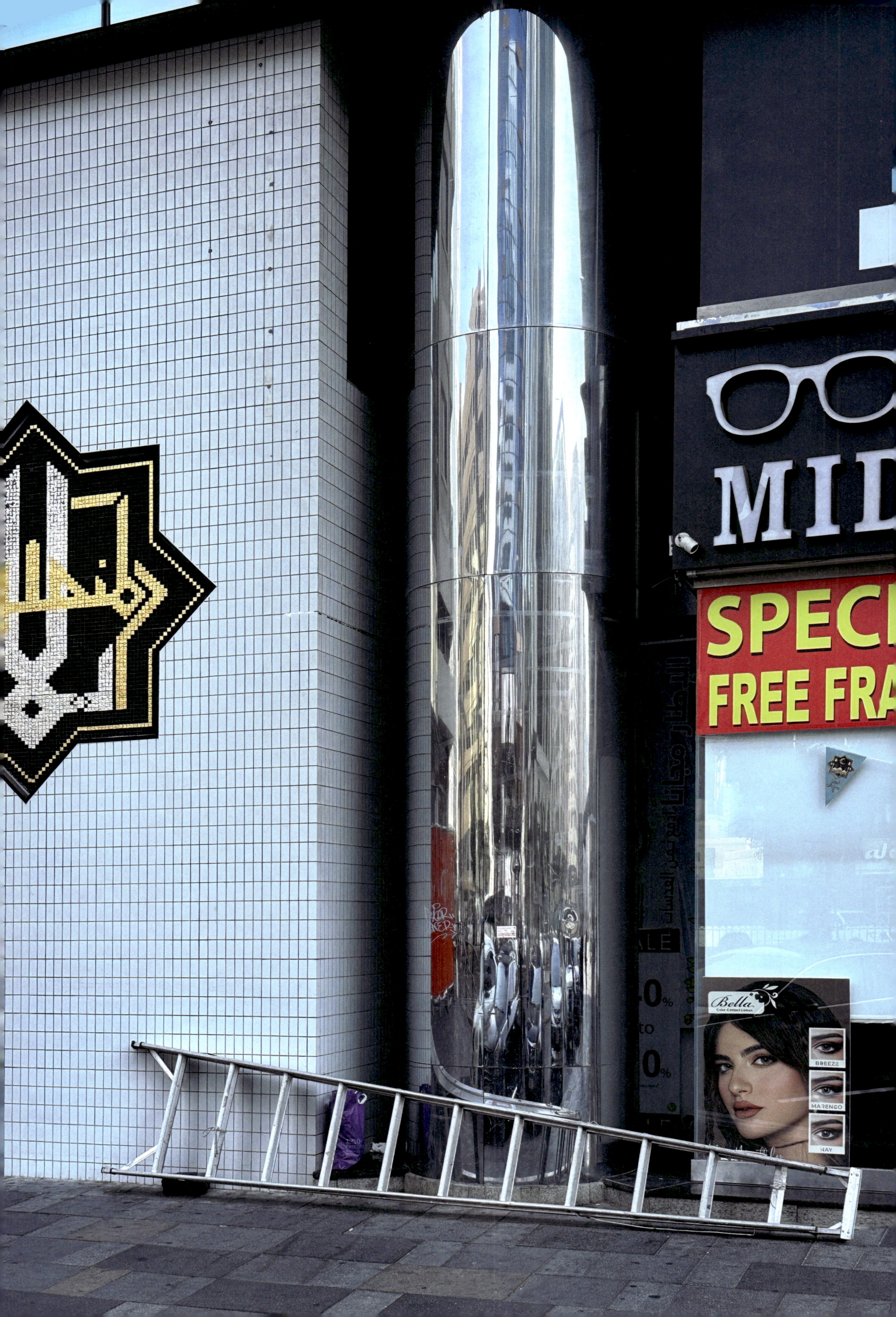

MID
SPECI
FREE FRA
Bella
BREEZE
MARENGO
RAY

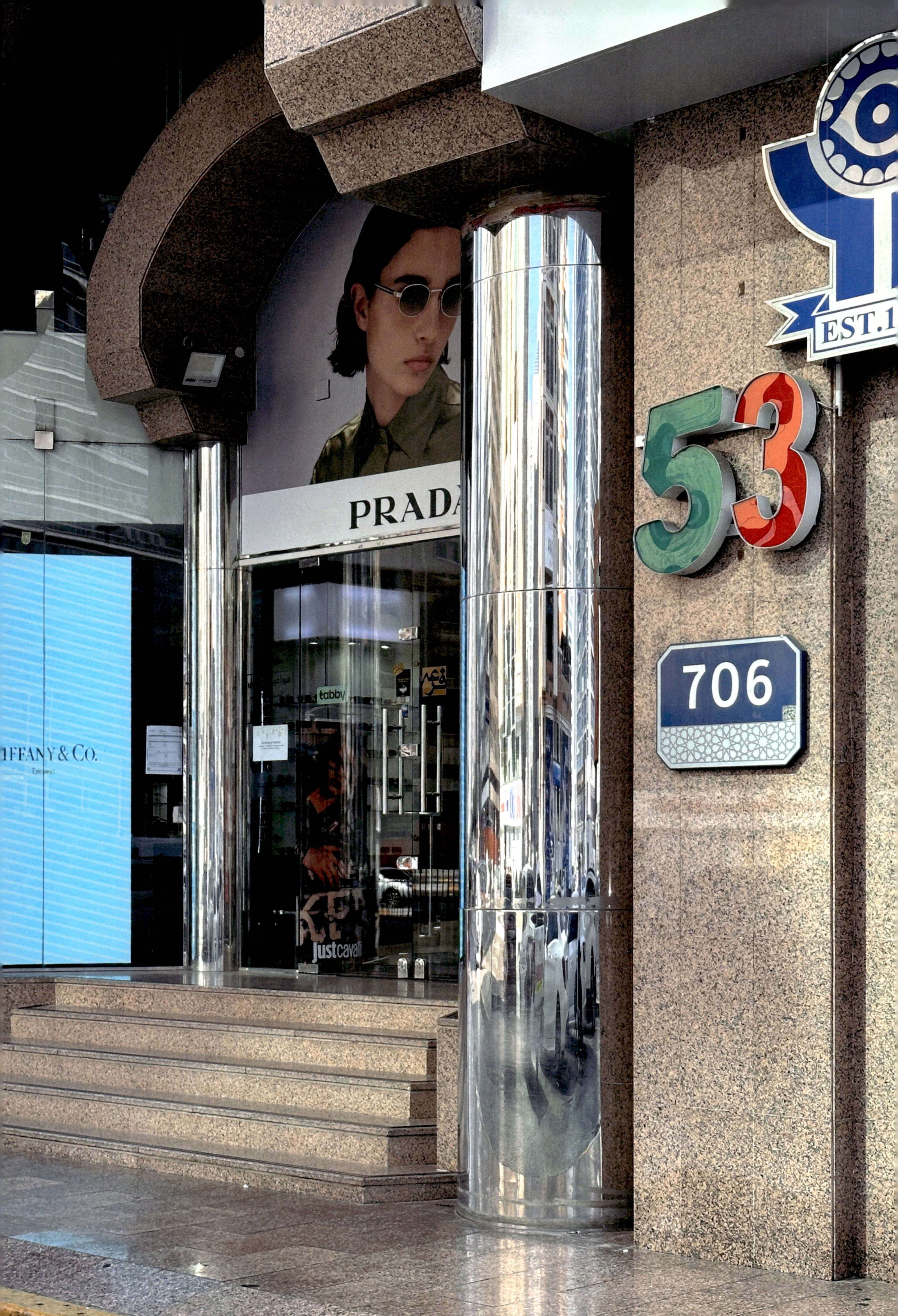

PRADA
TIFFANY & CO.
Eyewear
tabby
Justcavalli
53
EST.1
706

37

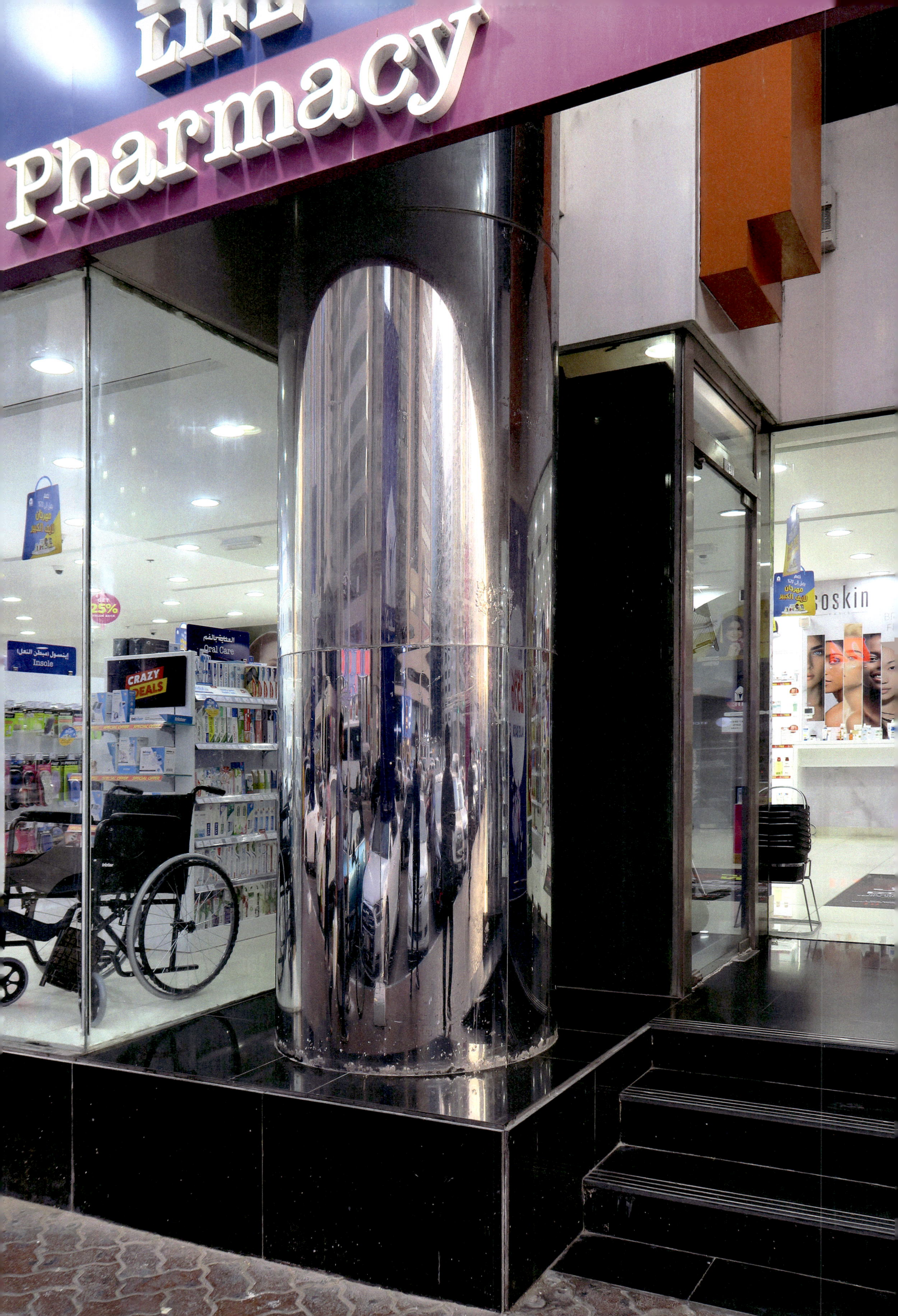

LIFE
Pharmacy
Insole
إبنسول (مبطن النعل)
Oral Care
العناية بالفم
CRAZY DEALS
GET 25%
soskin

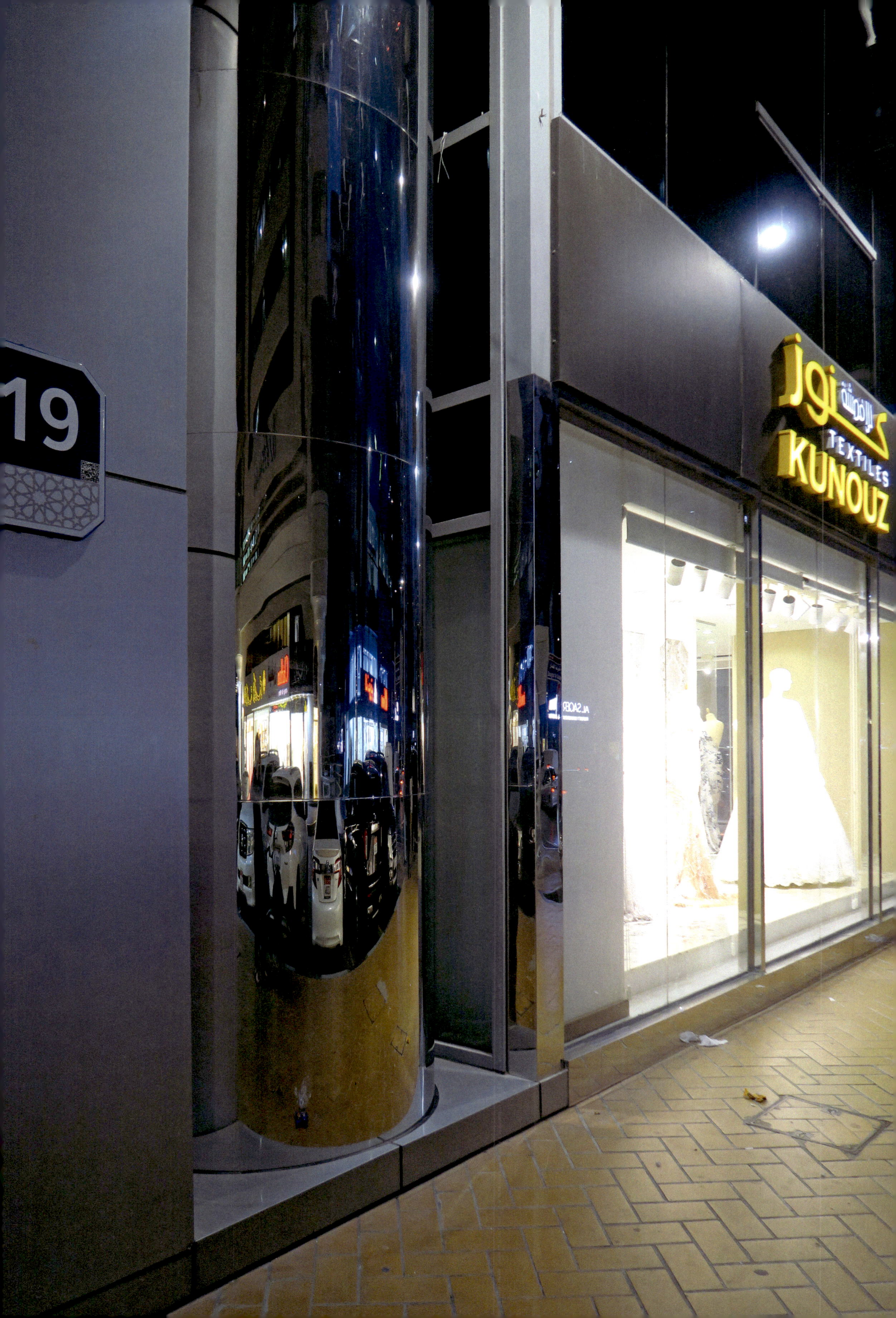

19
كنوز
TEXTILES
KUNOUZ

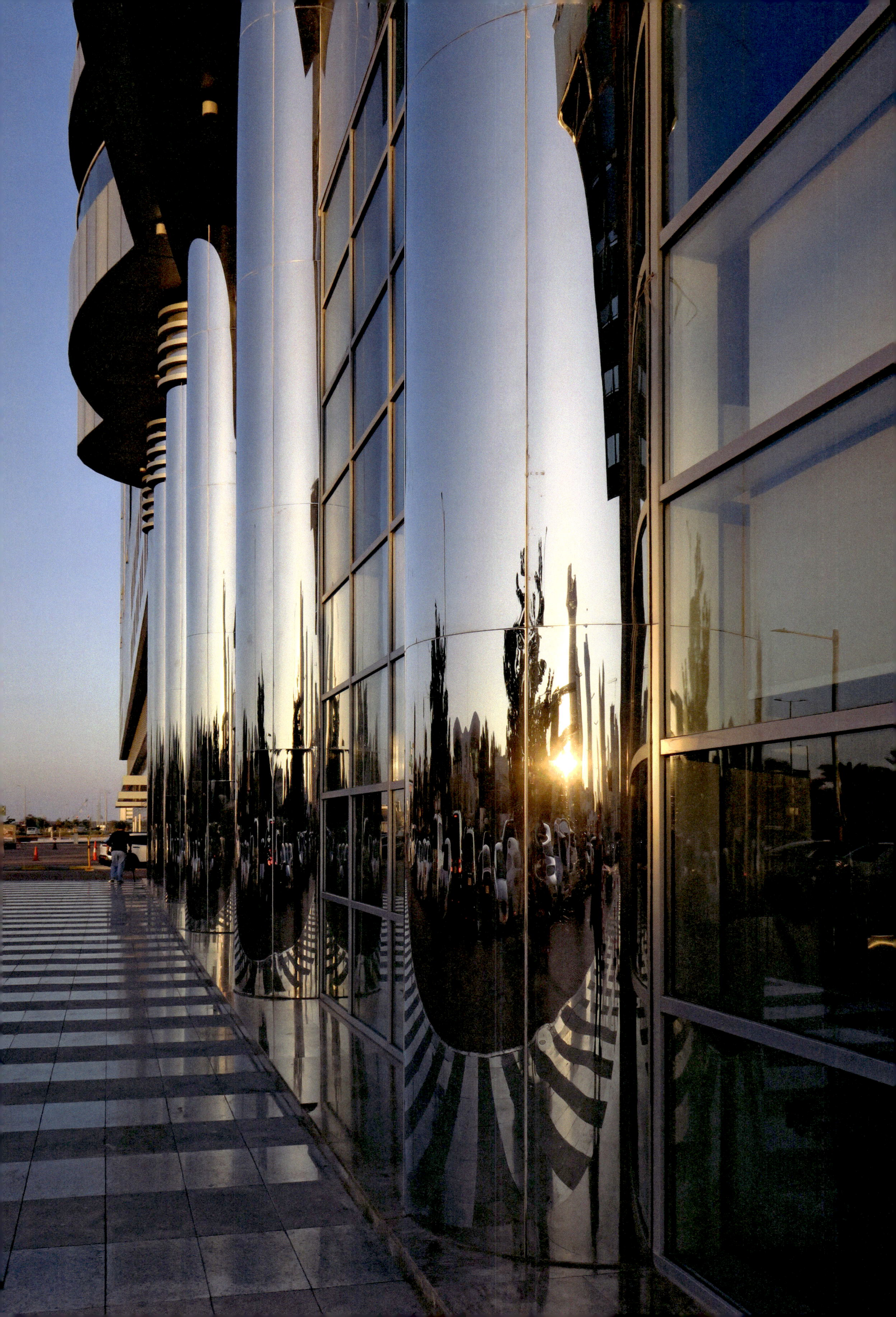

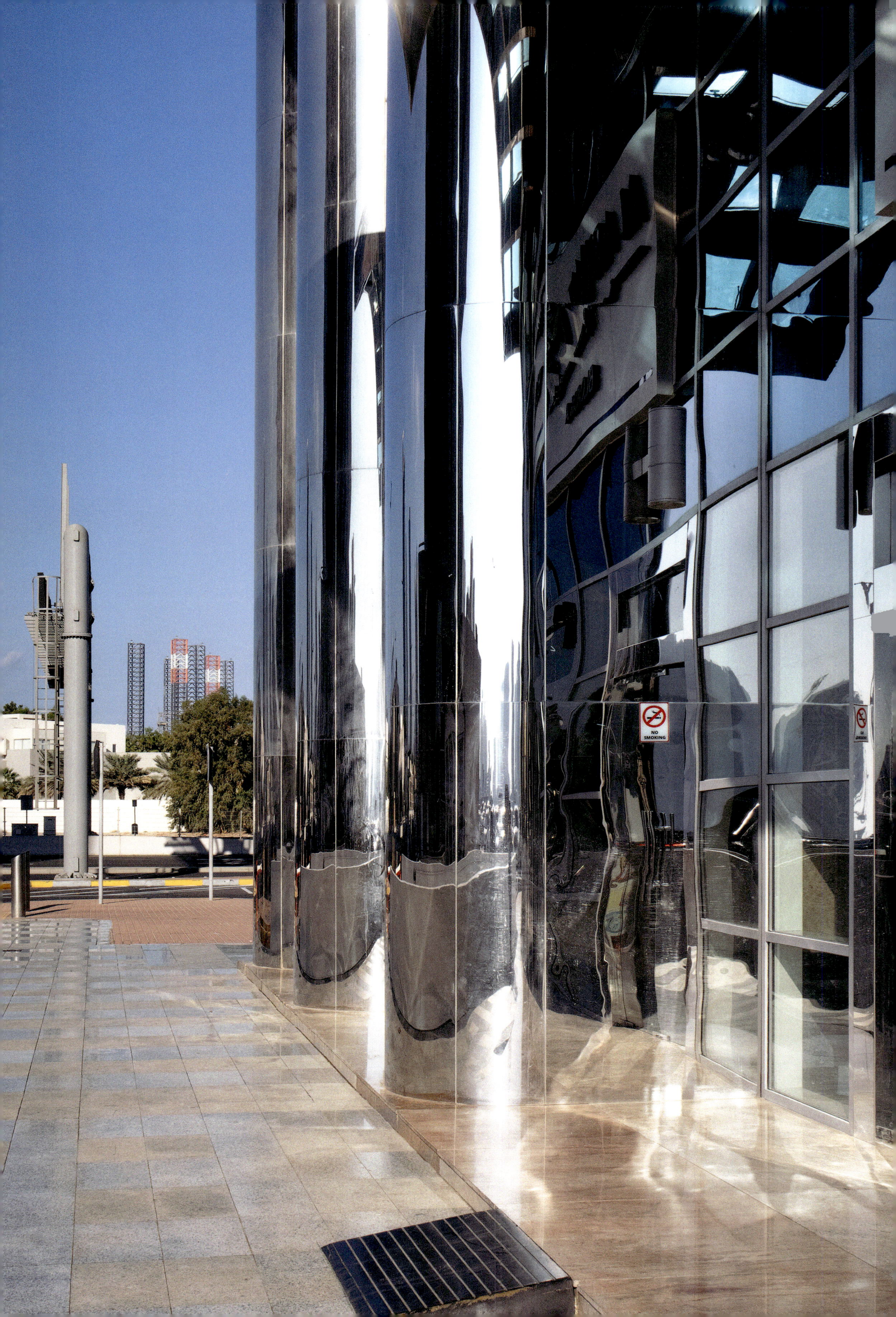
NO
SMOKING

41

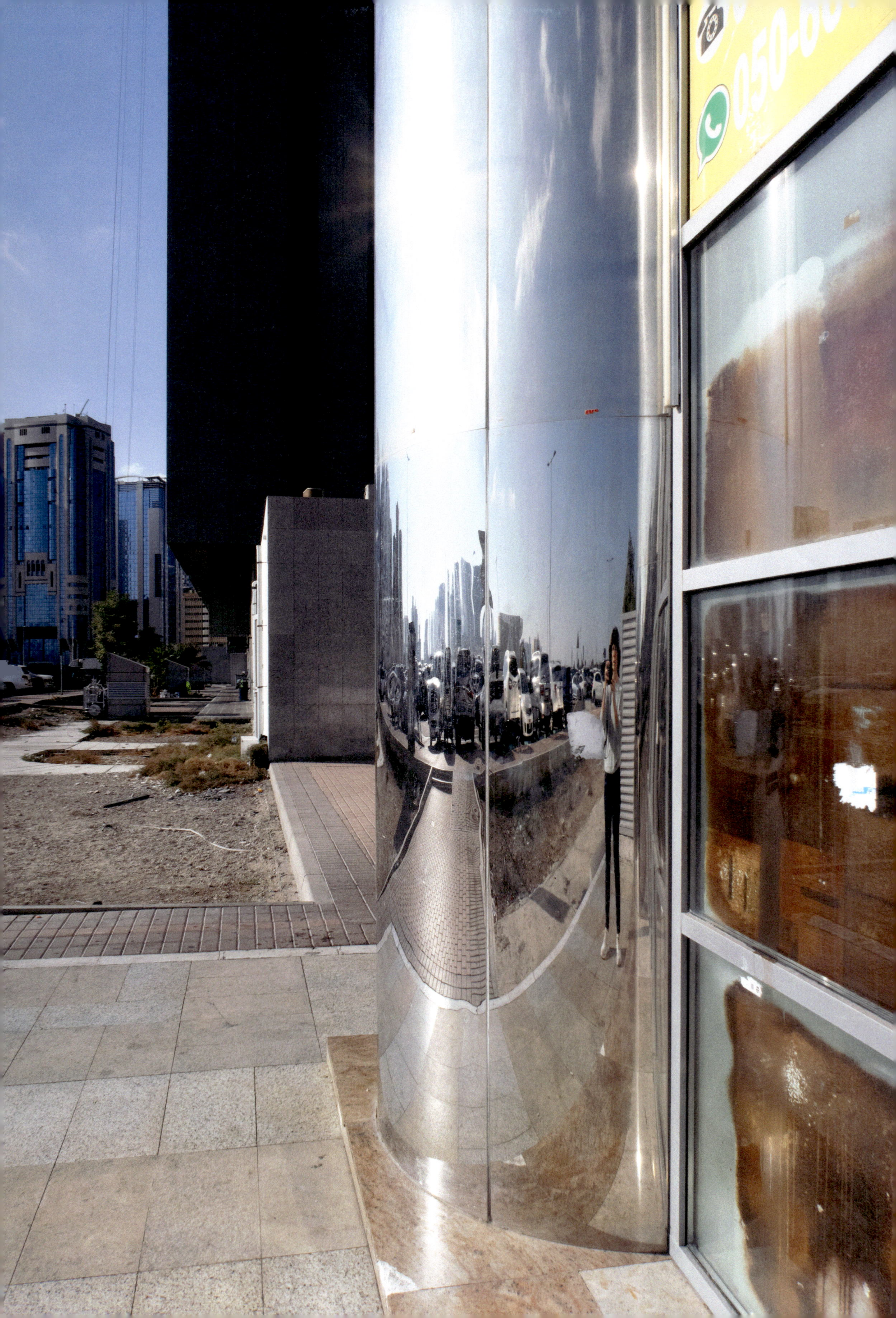

050-6

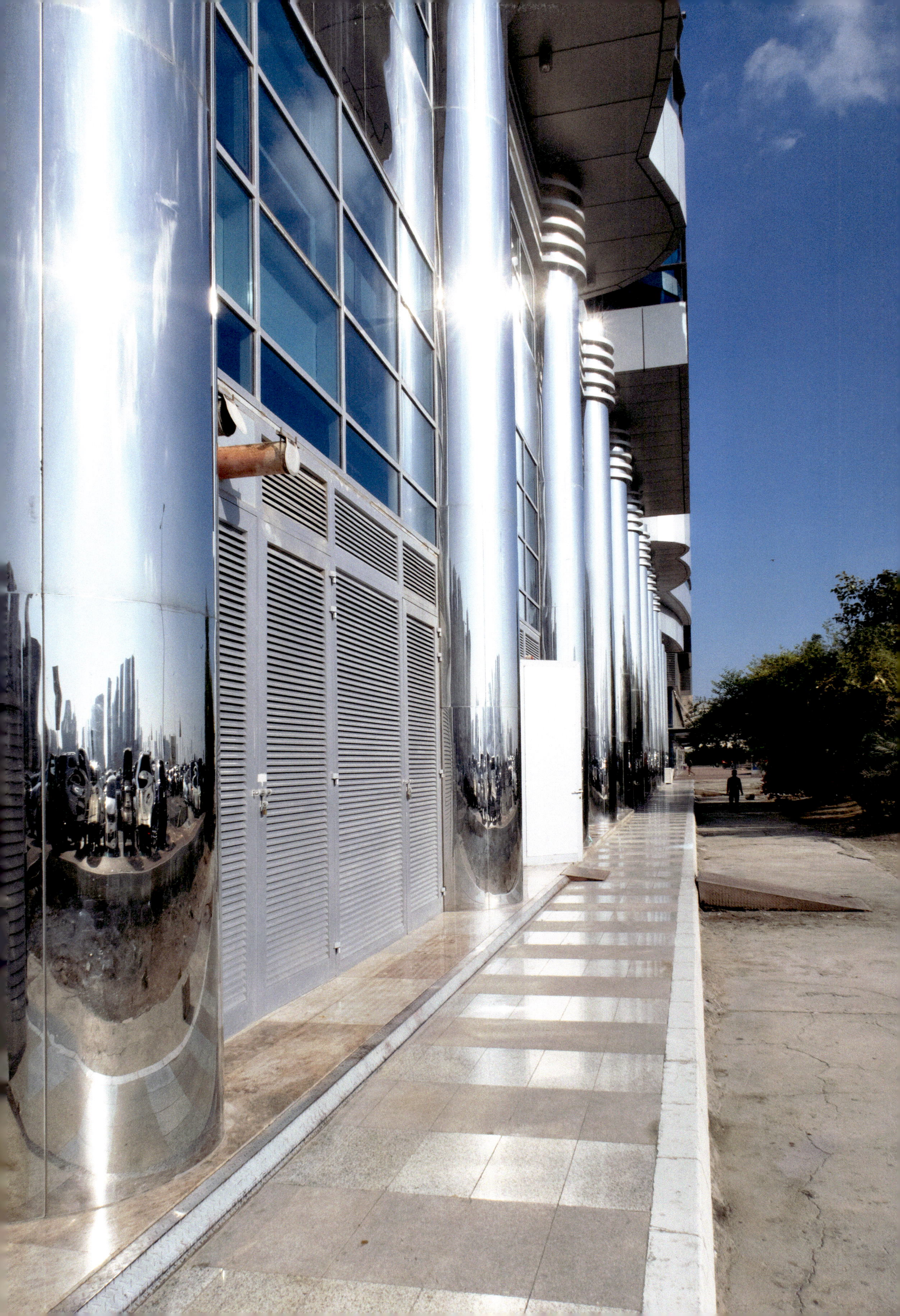

43

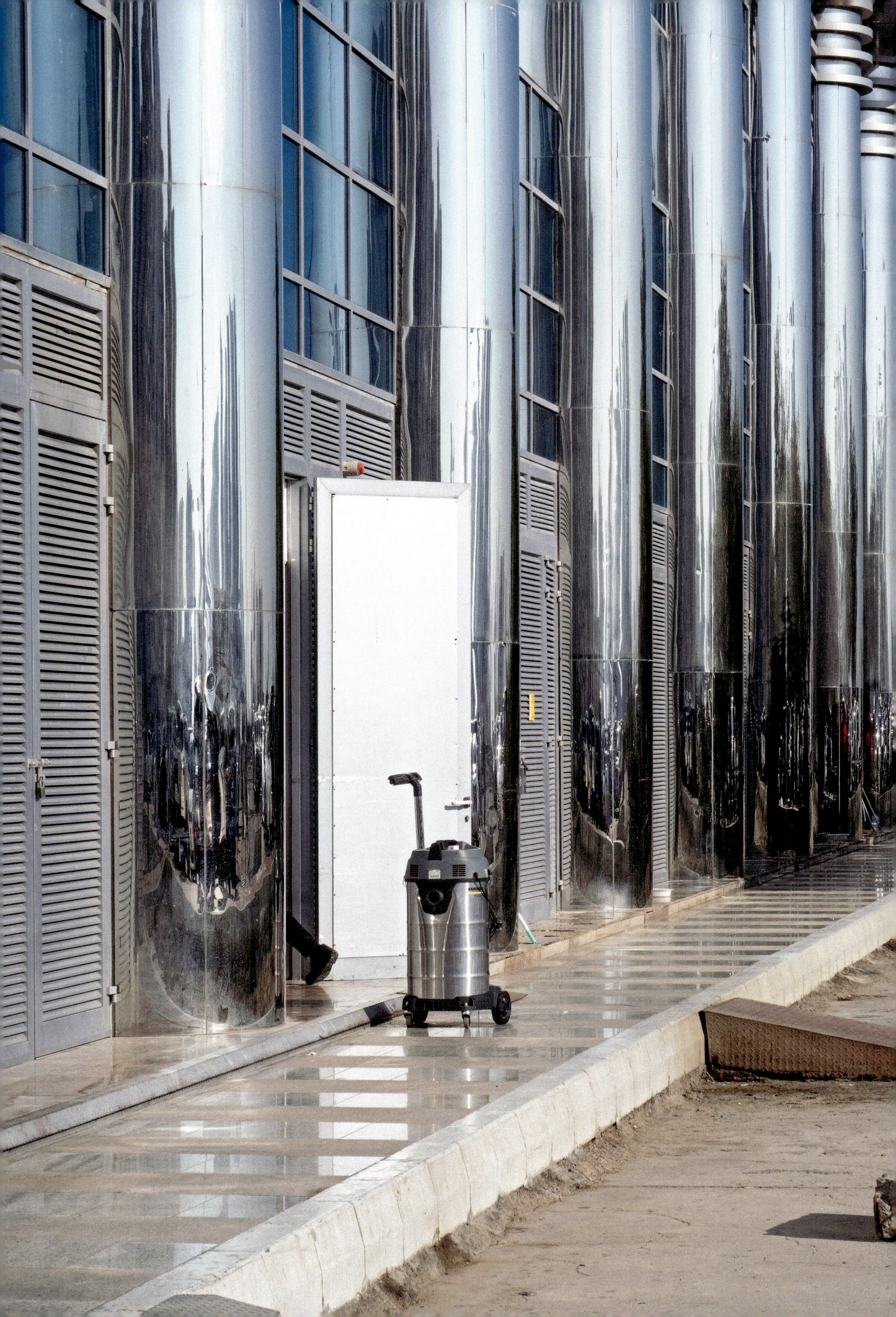

44

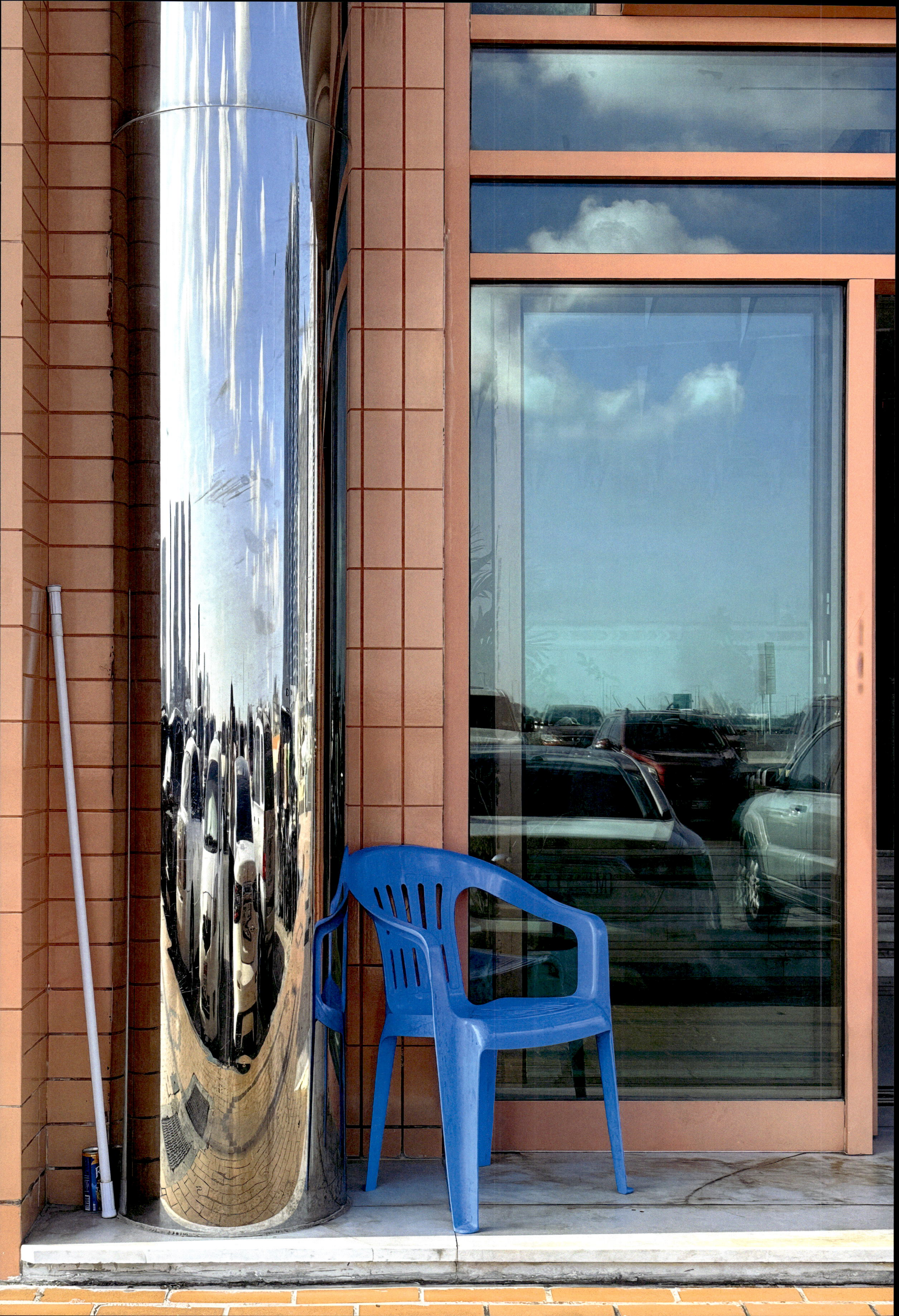

45

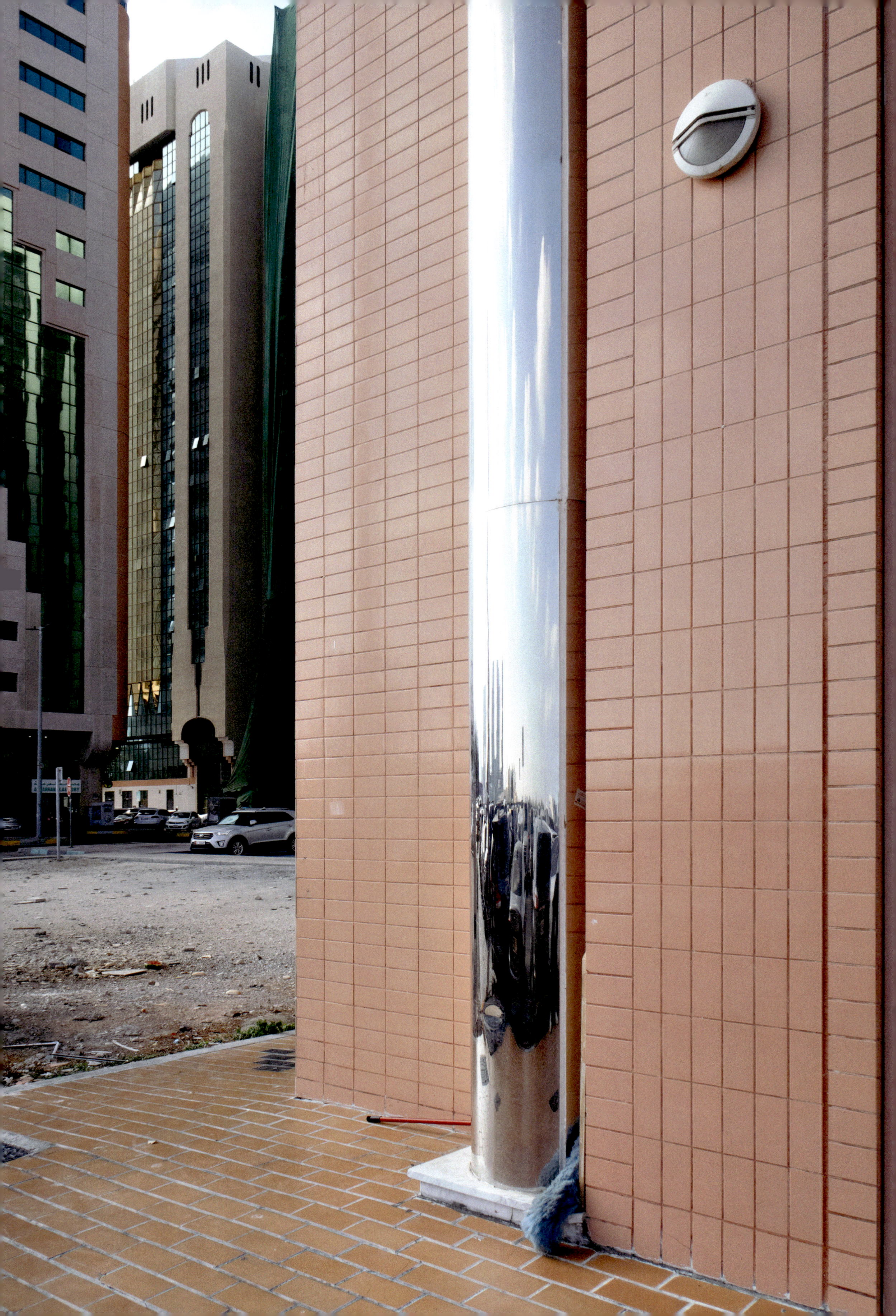

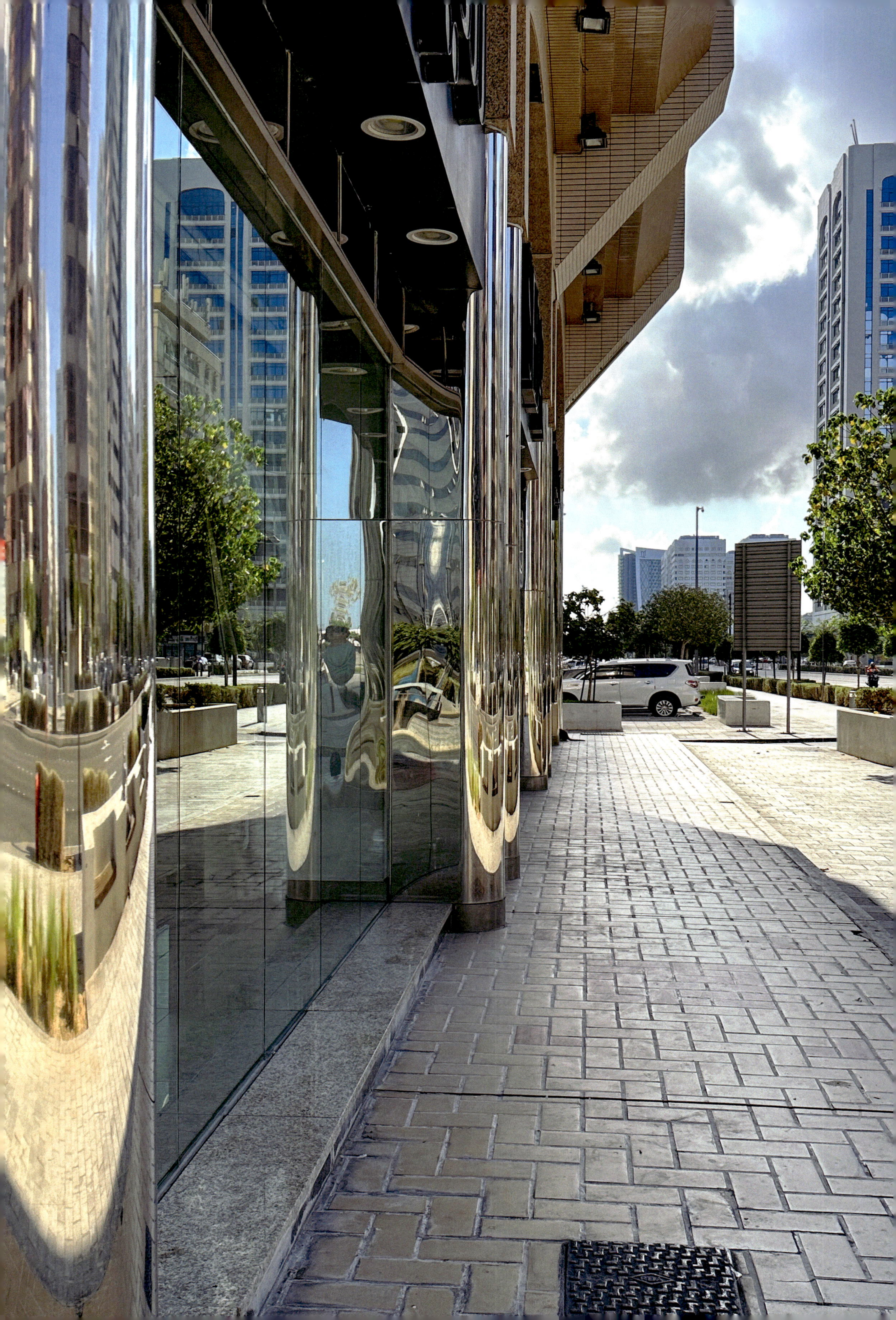

47

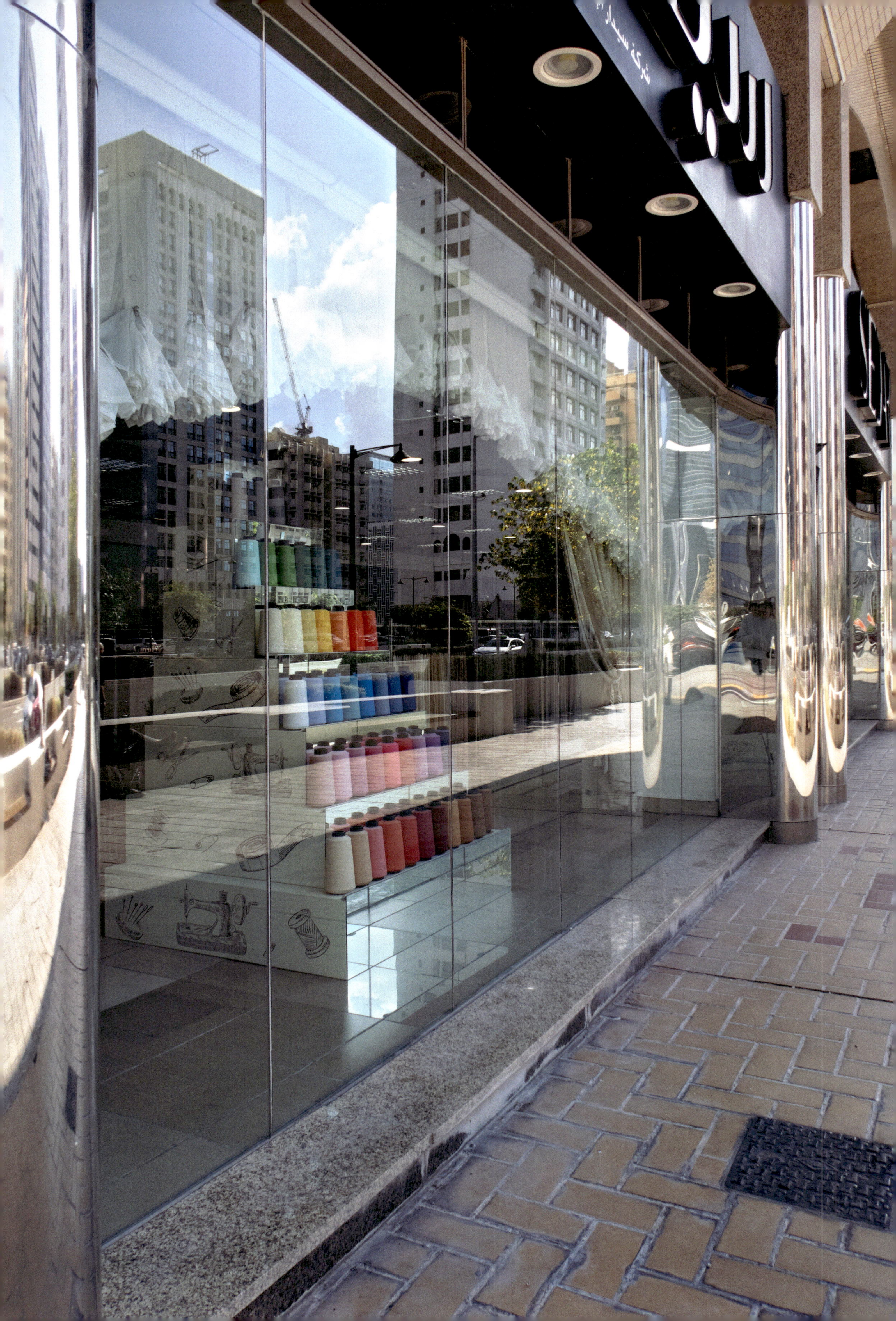

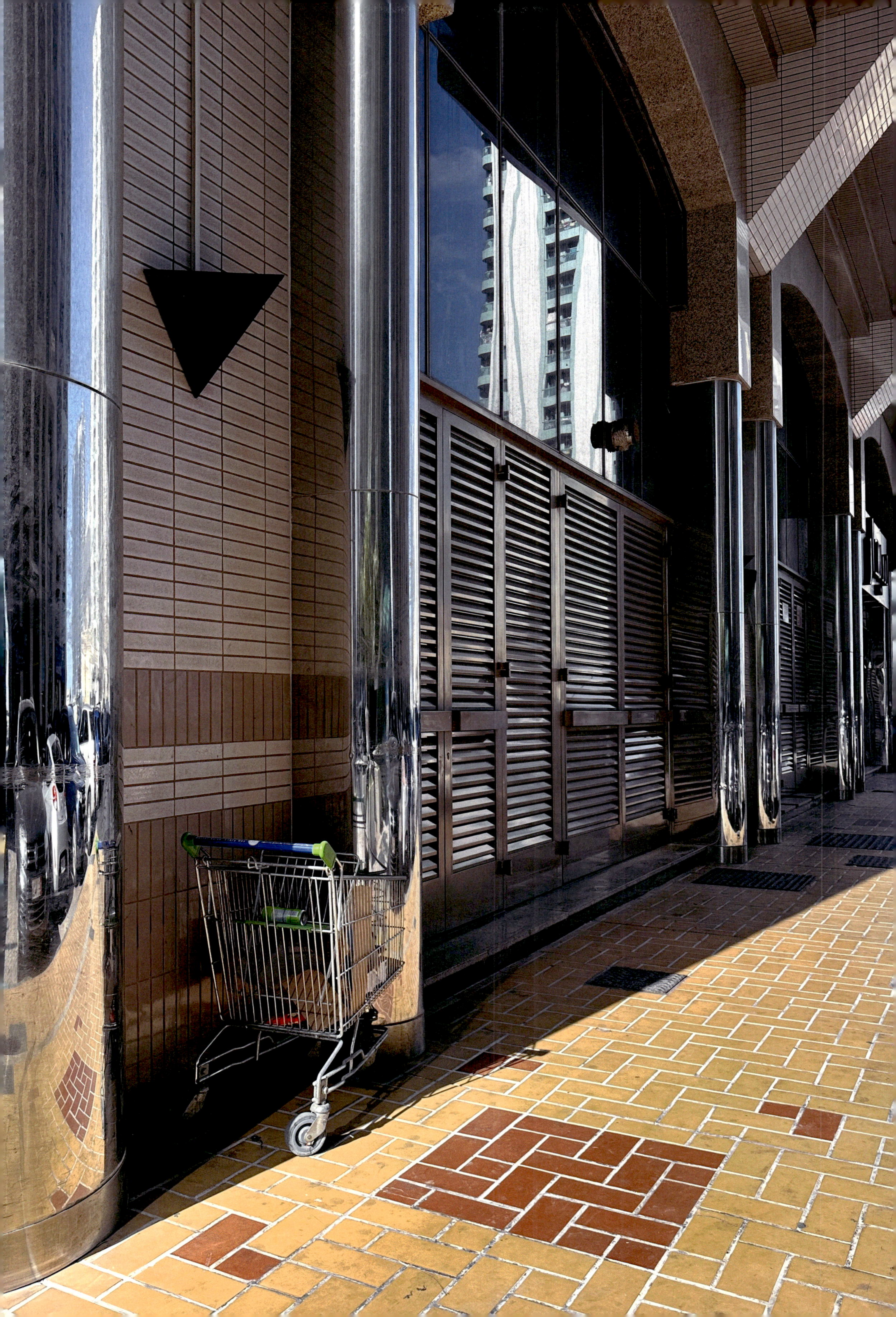

49

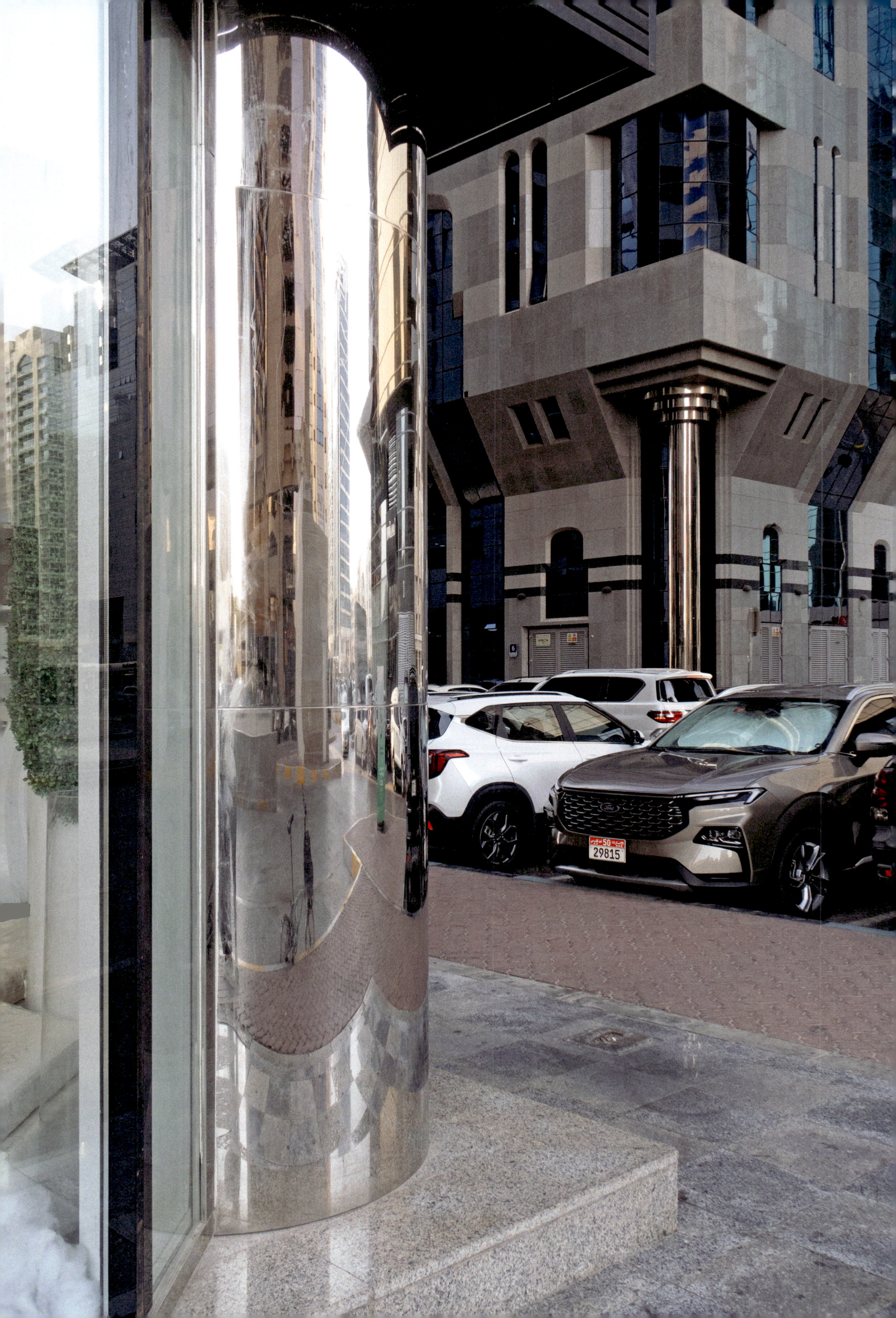

50

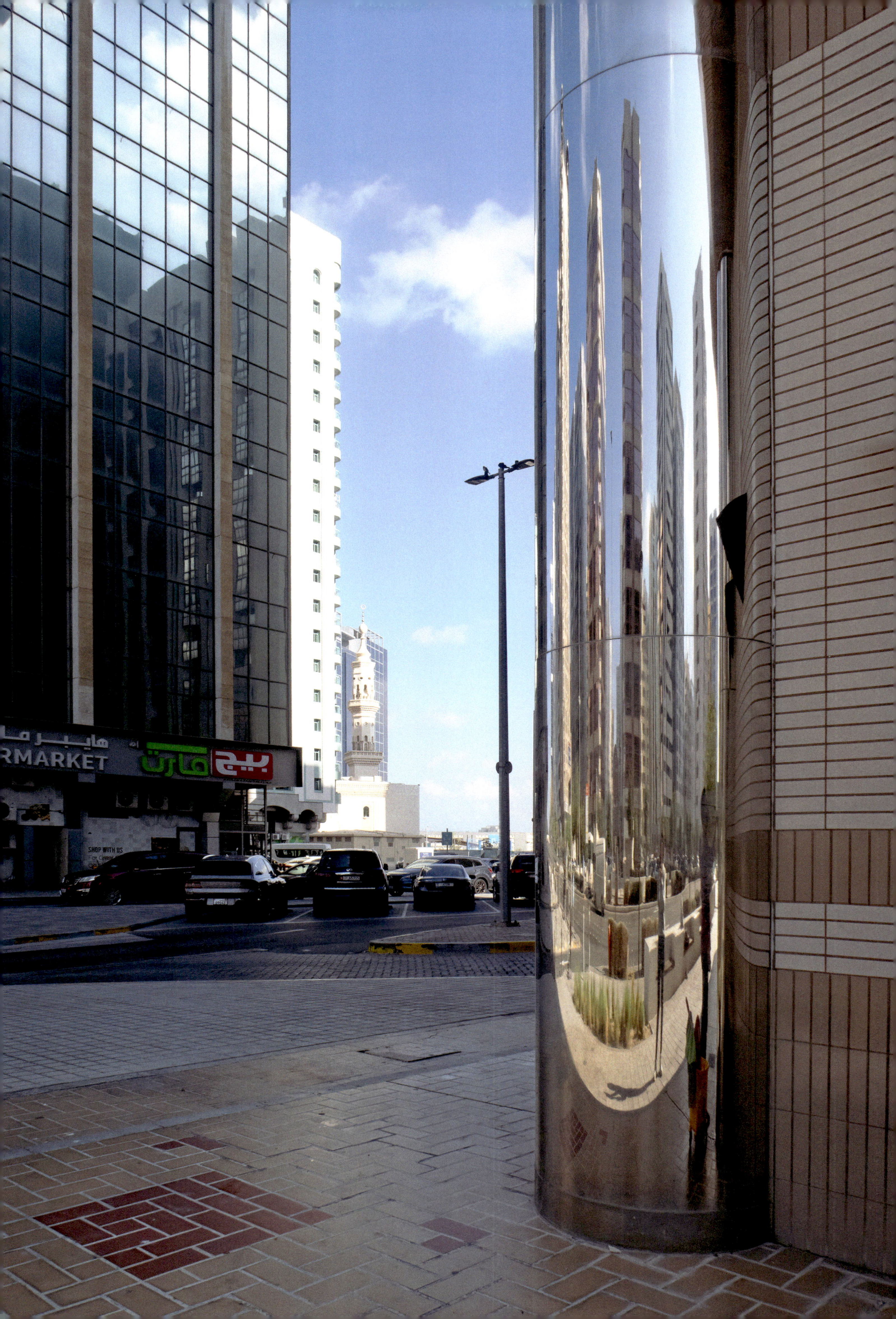
RMARKET
هايبر ما
بيج مارت
SHOP WITH US

51

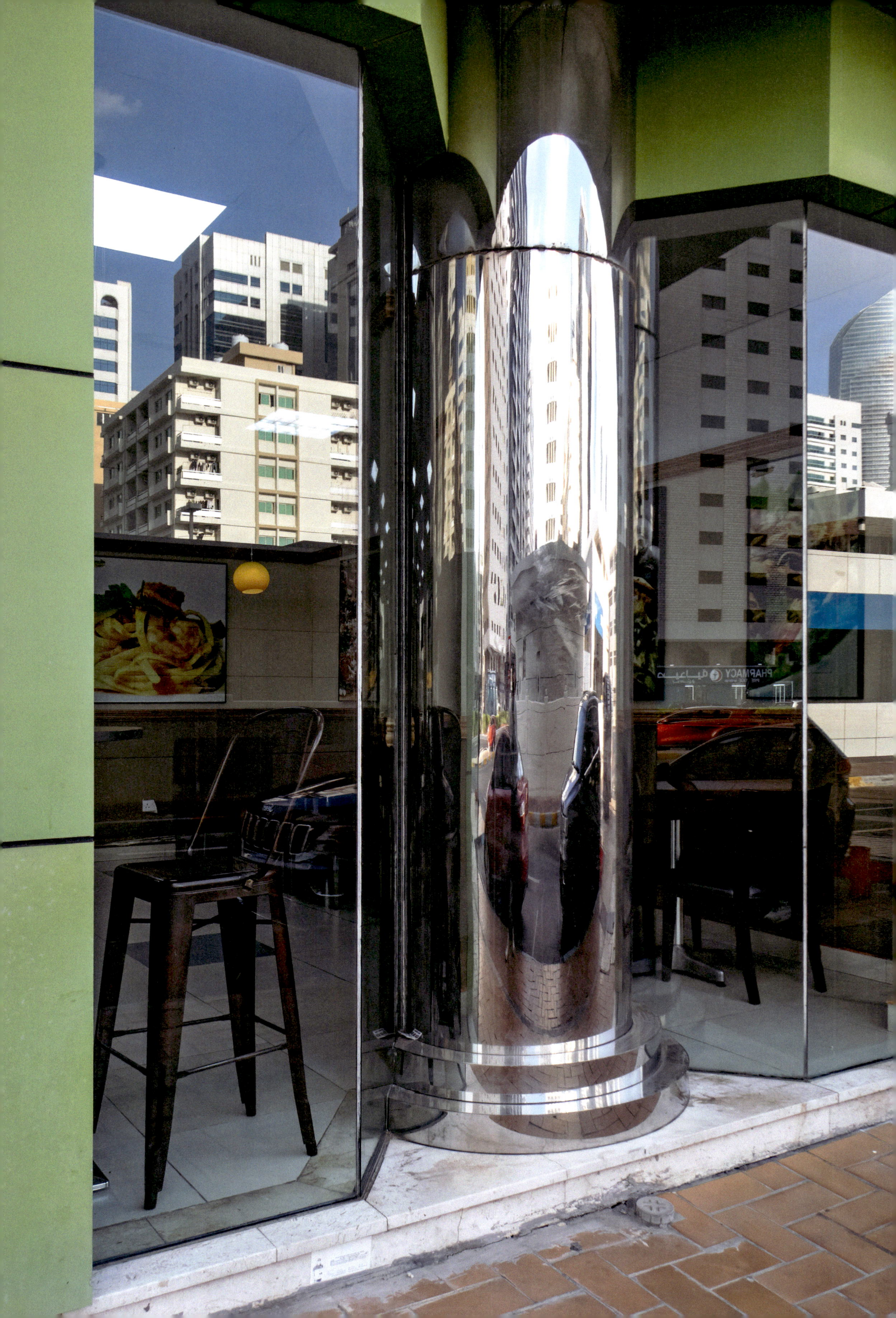

01
Al Yusr St.
Al Markaziyah
24.48941° N, 54.35486° E

02
Hamdan Bin Mohammed
St. 401
Al Markaziyah
24.48599° N, 54.35751° E

03
Hamdan Bin Mohammed
St. 399
Al Markaziyah
24.48601° N, 54.35715° E

04
Oud Maytha St. 17
Al Markaziyah
24.49060° N, 54.35666° E

05
Sheikh Rashid Bin Saeed
St. 109
Al Markaziyah
24.48949° N, 54.35444° E

06
Oud Maytha St. 17
Al Markaziyah
24.49062° N, 54.35665° E

07
Al Lulu St.
Al Danah
Al Markaziyah
24.2918° N, 54.21'52° E

08
Oud Maytha St. 17
Al Markaziyah
24.49062° N, 54.35665° E

09
Al Yusr St.
Al Markaziyah
24.49055° N, 54.35637° E

10
Oud Maytha St. 2/5
Al Markaziyah
24.49019° N, 54.35660° E

11
Al Yusr St.
Al Markaziyah
24.49044° N, 54.35642° E

12
Al Yusr St.
Al Markaziyah
24.49044° N, 54.35642° E

13
Al Yusr St.
Al Markaziyah
24.49055° N, 54.35637° E

14
Hamdan Bin Mohammed St.
Al Zahiyah
24.49792° N, 54.37465° E

15
Sheikh Zayed Bin Sultan St.
302
Al Markaziyah
24.49614° N, 54.37270° E

16
Sheikh Zayed Bin Sultan St.
302
Al Markaziyah
24.49608° N, 54.37260° E

17
Saeed Bin Ahmed Al Otaiba
St. 201
Al Markaziyah
24.49498° N, 54.36647° E

18
Saeed Bin Ahmed Al Otaiba
St. 201
Al Markaziyah
24.49498° N, 54.36647° E

19
Ramlat Bu Fraydah St. 4
Al Zahiyah
24.49847° N, 54.37446° E

20
Al Fakhr St. 24
Al Zahiyah
24.49934° N, 54.37569° E

21
Al Fakhr St. 24
Al Zahiyah
24.49934° N, 54.37569° E

22
Al Durri St.
Al Markaziyah
24.49470° N, 54.36916° E

23
Al Marakib St. 4
Al Markaziyah
24.48994° N, 54.35414° E

24
Hamdan Bin Mohammed
St. 808
Al Markaziyah
24.49730° N, 54.37483° E

25
Saeed Bin Ahmed Al Otaiba St.
Al Markaziyah
24.49370° N, 54.36699° E

26
Hamdan Bin Mohammed
St. 602
Al Markaziyah
24.48985° N, 54.36390° E

27
Hamdan Bin Mohammed
St. 606
Al Markaziyah
24.49034° N, 54.36456° E

28
Hamdan Bin Mohammed St.
Al Markaziyah
24.49329° N, 54.36841° E

29
Humaid Alhasm Al Rumaithi
St.
Al Markaziyah
24.49350° N, 54.36877° E

30
Hamdan Bin Mohammed St.
Al Markaziyah
24.49329° N, 54.36841° E

31
Iqam St. 7
Al Markaziyah
24.49779° N, 54.37428° E

32
Iqam St. 7
Al Zahiyah
24.49779° N, 54.37428° E

33
Hamdan Bin Mohammed
St. 525
Al Markaziyah
24.48978° N, 54.36316° E

34
Khalifa Bin Zayed The First
St. 318
Al Markaziyah
24.49123° N, 54.36070° E

35
Hamdan Bin Mohammed
St. 712
Al Markaziyah
24.49380° N, 54.36964° E

36
Safran St. 706
Al Markaziyah
24.49329° N, 54.36853° E

37
Hamdan Bin Mohammed
St. 602
Al Markaziyah
24.49021° N, 54.36430° E

38
Al Amtar St. 19
Al Danah
24.490285° N, 54.355982° E

39
Al Meena St. 254
Al Zahiyah
24.50698° N, 54.37649° E

40
Al Meena St 254
Al Zahiyah
24.50707° N, 54.37660° E

41
Al Meena St 254
Al Zahiyah
24.50701° N, 54.37658° E

42
Al Meena St 254
Al Zahiyah
24.50705° N, 54.37661° E

43
Al Meena St 254
Al Zahiyah
24.50705° N, 54.37661° E

44
Al Sindan St. 16
Al Zahiyah
24.50324° N, 54.37760° E

45
Al Sindan St. 16
Al Zahiyah
24.50321° N, 54.37764° E

46
Naseem Al Sharq St. 2
Al Zahiyah
24.50251° N, 54.37676° E

47
Naseem Al Sharq St. 2
Al Zahiyah
24.50248° N, 54.37677° E

48
Naseem Al Sharq St. 2
Al Zahiyah
24.50248° N, 54.37677° E

49
Al Mirqab St. 44/1
Al Khālidīyah
24.47381° N, 54.34701° E

50
Rizoum Jabir St. 2
Al Zahiyah
24.50247° N, 54.37679° E

51
Al Ghamrah St.
Al Ḥiṣn
24.47679° N, 54.35135° E

Index as of December 2025

Politics of Mirroring and Spaces of Imitation

George Katodrytis

Mirroring the world was invented in 600 BE by employing highly polished obsidian, which is a volcanic glass, as a reflective surface. It was during the Renaissance that Venetian manufacturers began making mirrors by applying a metallic surface to glass sheets. Since then, mirrors have become both decorative and utilitarian components in architecture, offering a clean, untainted, and modern aesthetic despite their archaic origins.

While both mirror and polished chrome surfaces reflect, chrome has taken the role of an aesthetic application and durable material, thus adopted by developers for interior and exterior use. Often called decor, it is applied as a surface to a facade, like the optical effects used in military camouflage. While the use of reflective surfaces in interiors can create the illusion of more space, their use on exteriors can have the opposite effect—creating an act of disappearance. While the interior appears bigger, the exterior becomes deconstructed. This visual disappearance of the facade can be interpreted in two, conflicting ways: as an enhancement and beautification of the urban streetscape, or to simulate random and distorted encounters within an oscillation between the shiny and the shabby.

The artist and academic Sandra Peters has observed and photographed the pattern of the subliminal effects of round, chrome-clad mirrored columns along the main building-block facades in downtown Abu Dhabi. These columns appear to be benign and are usually unnoticed by casual passersby. The columns are, in effect, invisible. They create patterns of distorted reflections, like abstract barcodes, of incomprehensible objects and disjointed human figures. In a dusty streetscape, these glossy surfaces erase building lines and well-defined edges, and remodel the city to a blurry, universal, and nonspecific reading of spaces. Peters wonders whether "the reflecting facades create an environment in which it becomes impossible for people to develop an actual identity in relation to place."

Mirror Complexities

1. Dan Graham's *Public Space/Two Audiences*, the first of the artist's so-called pavilions, was installed at the Venice Biennale in 1976.

2. Dan Graham, "Mirror Complexities," interview with Robert Enright and Meeka Walsh, *Bordercrossings*, December 2009, https://bordercrossingsmag.com/article/dan-graham-mirror-complexities.

3. Dan Graham, "Heart Pavilion" (1999), in *Two-Way Mirror Power: Selected Writings by Dan Graham on His Art*, ed. Alexander Alberro (Cambridge, MA: MIT Press, 1999), 173.

4. Alamira Reem Bani Hashim, *Planning Abu Dhabi* (London: Routledge, 2020), 241.

In his installation work *Public Space/Two Audiences* (1976),[1] the artist Dan Graham looked at the use of mirrors in creating borders, forming a complex experience in a public space. He noted: "It was based on a video piece I did for shop windows in an arcade, but here … I had people looking at each other in place of objects."[2] Similarly, Peters observes that "The reflections in the columns resemble the indirect gaze; they are mediators, without establishing genuine contact." Graham's critical engagement manifests most alluringly in his glass and mirrored pavilions. In these settings, the instruments of reflection—visual and cognitive—highlight the voyeuristic elements of design in the built world. He describes his work and its various manifestations as "geometric forms … inhabited and activated by the presence of the viewer, [producing] a sense of uneasiness and psychological alienation … by a constant play between feelings of inclusion and exclusion."[3] Such interactive communication may work in art installations, but is this binary alienation, exchange, and feeling of being inside and outside of images perceived as a novel street experience?

Reflections on the Planning of Abu Dhabi

The planning evolution of Abu Dhabi is a unique experiment in urbanization. Since the 1960s, the city has been struggling to maintain a contemporary expression that remains rooted in its own history of Arab urbanism. It has emerged as a hybrid model in the post-orientalist perspective. As Alamira Reem mentions in her book *Planning Abu Dhabi*, "Global and local processes are constantly being tested against each other as they play out (for example, the global expert working within the parameters of an overwhelmingly tribal structure) and as new urban typologies are being presented."[4]

The early plan of Abu Dhabi is based on an expandable rectangular grid of main and slip roads defining the edge of superblocks to house mainly migrant settlers. As Peters mentions in her text, "Abu Dhabi is based on a checkerboard plan that is further structured and characterized by superblocks." This system allowed for rapid expansion, both horizontally and vertically, and created repeated typologies of building volumes and facades. In subsequent revisions, the various master plans allowed for an expansion of plot sizes, which were increased to 60 × 80 ft (18 × 24 m) or other variations with a maximum size of 100 × 100 ft (30.5 × 30.5 m), to accommodate more buildings, with heights of eight to ten stories.

Several building types and designs have resulted from the guidelines and building regulations. Variations of decorative elements were used to compensate for the otherwise monotonous experience.

Reem mentions that "architectural pastiche" is coupled with the planning regulations that defined plot coverage, plots sizes, heights, setbacks, and allowable projections.[5] This inevitably produced a regular urban structure made up of a series of buildings with identical massing on similar plot subdivisions, with some diversity of uses but almost no sense of urbanism.

A significant and abrupt shift took place between 2000 and 2005, when new buildings or remodeling of existing ones saw the sudden introduction of reflective glass, chrome, and aluminum cladding. The urgency of the city to be "modernized," together with the abundance of aluminum extrusion factories in the UAE, made these materials more readily available, locally produced, cheap, and fashionable. It was an easy solution to face-lift the skin of the city. Ceramic tiling also began to appear on facades. Another trend that was influenced by Western design was the curtain glass walling. The city's first curtain wall building emerged in 1989 on the Abu Dhabi Corniche, the first building to be completely curtain walled with curved glass and panoramic elevations.

Lacan's Mirror and the Mask: Psychoanalysis and the City

Is the mirror in the city an exploration of space or a distraction? As one moves in front of that mirror, something uncanny happens: there is a distorted and parallel movement. At first glance, it is disorienting, but also quite playful. The artist Anish Kapoor questions this: "What am I looking at? Is it another void object, a non-object?"[6] Such an experience is suggestive of the mirror stage theory, developed by French psychoanalyst Jacques Lacan, which describes the developmental stage when a young child starts to identify its own image in a mirror and starts to make crude distinctions between the self and the other when it sees its reflection. Lacan also evokes the idea of a fantasized gaze, referring to the gaze as a cause of visual fascination. This gaze magnetizes the eye, inspiring "the feeling of strangeness" whereby the subject under the gaze is "caught, manipulated, captured, in the field of vision," not dissimilar to the phenomenon of animal mimicry, where the visual settings and cones of vision operate in a way that "the subject is not completely aware of it."[7]

5. Reem, *Planning Abu Dhabi*, 154. As she notes, her use of the term is via Abbad Al Radi.

6. Sonia Kolesnikov-Jessop, "Anish Kapoor on the Power of Concave Mirrors," Cobosocial. com, May 28, 2019, https:// www.cobosocial.com/dossiers/ anish-kapoor-on-the-power- of-concave-mirrors/.

7. Lacan as quoted in Maria Scott, "Deciphering the Gaze in Lacan's 'Of the Gaze as Objet Petit a,'" in *The DS Project: Image, Text, Space/Place, 1830–2015*, https://hdl.handle.net/ 10871/17737.

We must accept that a chrome-clad column as an object exists twice:
first as a physical existence of itself, and second as representation.
As such, the outside of this thing (representation) must include
the inside of a thing (existence). The exterior of a building is a
spatial moment represented as an image of a casual reflection and
encounter. It is always in contradiction. It is what represents the
building to a subject. The assertion that an object exists twice,
as representation and as existence, does not aim to divide the object
into two aspects. It involves the causal proposition that, if the
representational order of the object overcoats its existence, it also
determines the fantasy of what the inside is.

It might be possible to "see" something that isn't there, just as it is
possible to see something that is there. All manner of distortion
might be allowed to fall between the act of seeing and the facts of
what is there—distortions that would fall somewhere between
hallucination and abstraction. But to stare at something which is
not there seems to make no sense. How could we tolerate such an
underdetermined world where one can stare at what is not there?
The existence of objects, and the modalities of their existence, must
be viewed not exclusively from the point of view of presence but
from the point of view of its "ghost"—the negative world of inverse
objects.

If the face ceases to express, the exterior ceases to signify. What is
left is a mere mask. And a mask cannot contain existence. It no
longer produces the effect of depth. Buildings which are given a
face-lift of distracting detail also prove that masks cannot signify.
What is presenting itself here is a de-signifying device whereby
the subject retreats to a repertoire of acts of turning away, of hiding,
and of vanishing. In effect, we block our eyes, and we turn away.
But what characterizes such defenses is not so much that they
provide certain kinds of experience but that they suspend the experience of objects. Experience is neutralized in favor of indifference.

Within the pragmatic continuum of our everyday affairs, we remain
mostly indifferent to our surroundings. We may take into conside-
ration the philosophical account of beauty and ugliness that was
laid down in antiquity. For Plato, the beautiful object is one that has
the ideal structure of an object; it embodies totality. The art object
must be articulated, which is assumed to reveal its essence. This
implied two things that were equally unthinkable. It would amount
to a contradiction in terms to speak of an infinite whole. With
regards to the chromed columns, one experiences a paradoxical play
with the unthinkable. The mirrored surface of the column makes it
impossible to see it as a formally self-contained gestalt, or the

8. For more on ugliness,
see Mark Cousins, *The Ugly I,
II, III* (Santiago: ARQ, 2020),
which collects the architectural
theorist's 1994–95 AA Files
articles on the subject.

whole. One can at best look at the connection of column and ground to gain some understanding of an existing object and its location. The ancient Greek ideas of beauty and ugliness involved speculative metaphysical concepts concerning their relation to truth and reality. An ugly object was considered a negation not just of beauty, but of truth, a negation of reality, too. Ugliness belonged to whatever negates that truth. It belonged to a series of categories that similarly distort the truth of objects.[8] Looking at the chromed columns with such categories in mind is a possibility that can only lead to a negative assessment. One could counter this by realizing that in the modern period, it became possible that artworks exposed ugliness to mirror an already ugly reality, to tell the truth about it. But this can't be said about the chromed columns of Abu Dhabi. They seem to reject both possibilities, showing an indifference to the metaphysical ideas that are involved in them, in favor of using and exposing an enlivening spectacularization of the spectacular.

Paradoxically, the adding of thin chrome mirror cladding on columns has disjointed the facade from its object (building) and context (setting). The boundaries and hard edges of buildings as things have been erased and transformed to a streetscape of kaleidoscopic and chaotic experience. The medium is not the message anymore. The city's historical organization of planning and of expansion has been dismantled.

When the architecture of the permanence and the motionless becomes fluid, the building ceases to be a reference object and an anchor; It dissolves in the world of superfluous simulations and incomprehensible effects, and it threatens our spatial experience. The city becomes entertaining and merely shallow and superficial. It may, though, offer a unique opportunity for new urban interventions. Peters writes of the shift in her perception enabling her to "look at a column in the cityscape and see it as a sculptural object without isolating it from its existing context." The municipality and building owners could be inventive and decide to make proposals to separate and detach the reflective surfaces from the body of the building and turn them to urban furniture, installations, and street utilities along the sidewalks of the main streets. This would allow buildings to be liberated from the burden of their representation and once again return to their existential, formal, material, raw, and solid state while simultaneously allowing the streetscape to exist as a playful urbanism.

Sandra Peters

Sandra Peters is an artist, writer, and educator based in Abu Dhabi, UAE. She was born in 1969 in Bonn, Germany. In 2001, she earned a PhD in the Arts from the Hochschule für Bildende Künste in Dresden. Before her studies, she completed an apprenticeship as a goldsmith.

Peters's work focuses on architecture and urban space, aiming to achieve integration of and reciprocity between sensual, structural, and conceptual elements. Her first project related to architecture, titled *Modification—Constantly Climbing Stones*, was exhibited in 2009 at Kunstverein Ruhr in Germany.

She has presented her work extensively in institutions and project spaces across Europe, the United States, and the United Arab Emirates. Her books include *CutCube* (2022) and *PER/TRANS: Performing the Cube, Transforming the Cube. Works by Sandra Peters, 1998–2017* (2018).

Since 2014, Peters has been teaching in the Art and Art History Program at New York University Abu Dhabi, where she served as Co-Program Head from 2021 to 2025.

George Katodrytis

George Katodrytis is an architect involved in practice, teaching and research. He is Professor of Architecture at the College of Architecture, Art and Design of the American University of Sharjah since 2001 and was Head of the Department of Architecture from 2017 to 2023.

He studied and taught at the Architectural Association School of Architecture. He also taught at the Bartlett School of Architecture, University College London. He has been a visiting professor at various schools around the world. He has built several projects in Europe and published widely on contemporary architecture, urbanism, cultural theory, and digital media. Much of his work addresses the "Gulf City," especially as it is evolving in the twenty-first century. He employs digital technology and scripting as tools for establishing new formal and performative language and materiality. He was the coeditor of the *Architectural Design* special issue "UAE and the Gulf: Architecture and Urbanism Now."

Sandra Peters
Chromed Columns / Abu Dhabi City

Concept:
Sandra Peters and
Heimann + Schwantes

Design:
Heimann + Schwantes

Translations from German:
Gerrit Jackson

Copyediting:
Alexander Scrimgeour,
Amanda Brooks Heintz

Digital Imaging:
Prints Professional
Jan Scheffler & Kerstin Wenzel GbR

Paper:
GardaPat 13 Bianca
Munken Print White 15
Sirio Color

Printing and binding:
DZA Druckerei zu Altenburg GmbH

© 2026 for the reproduced works
by Sandra Peters: VG Bild-Kunst, Bonn

ISBN: 978-3-7757-6221-2

All rights reserved, including the rights
of reproduction and of translation, in
whole or in part.

Distribution worldwide by
Hatje Cantz Verlag GmbH
Mommsenstraße 27, 10629 Berlin
www.hatjecantz.de
A Ganske Publishing Group Germany

The publication is generously funded
by the NYUAD Faculty Research Grant
for the Arts and the NYUAD Grant for
Publication Support, New York University
Abu Dhabi, UAE.

The automated analysis of this publication in order to obtain information,
in particular about patterns, trends, and
correlations as outlined in § 44b ("Text
and data mining") of the German Act on
Copyright and Related Rights (UrhG),
is prohibited.

Printed in Germany